The Book of Pleasure
in Plain English

To my loyal friends

The Book of Pleasure in Plain English

being
The Book of Pleasure (Self-love);
The Psychology of Ecstasy

by
Austin Osman Spare

Elucidated by
C. J. Chibnall

Green Magic

The Book of Pleasure in Plain English
© 2014 Christopher Chibnall

Green Magic
5 Stathe Cottages
Stathe
Somerset TA7 0JL
England

info@greenmagicpublishing.com
www.greenmagicpublishing.com

ISBN 978 0 9566197 9 2

Green Magic

Deisgned and typeset by **K.DESIGN**, Somerset

Contents

Author's Preface

It has been said that whilst the writings of Austin Osman Spare have been translated (amazingly!) into a number of foreign languages, they have yet to be translated into English. The book you hold in your hands represents an attempt to do exactly that with his most important work: the *Book of Pleasure*. It started as a personal project to understand Spare's extraordinary, fascinating, yet frustrating *magnum opus*. It is intended as a maverick, semi-scholarly work, and does not pretend to be perfect. It should not be regarded as a substitute for the original, but only as a way towards understanding it.

The original *Book of Pleasure* is a great, odd, and truly magical book: although only fifty-nine pages long, including illustrations, one seems to find something new every time one re-reads it. It is written in a terse, convoluted style with numerous archaisms and neologisms, a strange use of syntax, and occasional sentences without verbs: few people ever get beyond the first couple of pages. At the same time, it gives the strong impression that there are ideas within it that are well worth understanding. Spare seems to have followed the example of the ancient Taoist philosophers, who made their texts deliberately obscure, forcing their readers to work at them, the theory being that people tend to value something they have worked for.

In addition to this, though, some of Spare's obscurity appears to be *un*intentional: he seems to have had a genuine difficulty with grammar, perhaps as a result of his working-class background and limited schooling. Two of his later writings, the *Focus of Life* and *Anathema of Zos*, appear to have been at least partly automatic in inspiration, and some passages in the *Book of Pleasure* may be. It is worth noting that grammatical ambiguity is characteristic of Ericksonian hypnotic language: I submit that some passages in Spare may not only have been written in trance, but also aim to induce trance or change state in the reader: the section on 'Paradox' in Spare's late work *The Living Word of*

Zos seems to confirm that he had (paradoxically!) a sophisticated knowledge of the suggestive possibilities of language.

The *Book of Pleasure* is written partly in prose, partly in poetry, and Spare is often at his clearest when writing poetically: this has been fortuitous, as I have often been able to leave his most poetic passages almost unchanged, and can hope to avoid the accusation of 'de-poeticising' Spare. For those, on the other hand, who may complain that I have not changed *enough* to make the exercise worthwhile, I can only hope they find that the end-notes go some way towards making up for this. I do urge *all* my readers to read the end notes: they are an important part of the book.

In her introduction to *Zos Speaks!* Steffi Grant states, 'Even what may – in print – seem the most curious constructions, become perfectly lucid when one recalls such sentences being voiced by him'. With this in mind, I have gone to some effort to track down a recording of a wireless interview that Spare gave the B.B.C. in 1955, but to no avail: regrettably, it seems to have gone the way of all too much of that institution's recorded heritage. However, Steffi Grant's statement does imply that Spare's sentences become clearer when spoken with a careful use of inflection or emphasis:

indeed, I have found that many of them are improved by simple changes in punctuation, and I have frequently used italics for emphasis.

The *Book of Pleasure in Plain English* has ended up considerably longer than the original. This is because the original is in a very terse style, in which a lot is implied rather than stated openly; I have made the text, I hope, clearer by 'teasing out' this implied meaning. In addition, I have felt the need to reduce Spare's rich vocabulary to a more limited range of standard words that reflect their more modern and familiar equivalents. Rather like the *Good News Bible*, I anticipate that this book will stand accused by some critics of negating the richness of the original language, and of 'dumbing down': I will have respect for those same critics if they are able to discuss Spare's ideas as a result of having read the original themselves from cover to cover.

I have heard the opinion expressed that the notion of a Sparean magical system is a myth, on the grounds that Spare discontinues his use of the terms 'Zos' and 'Kia' soon after finishing the *Book of Pleasure*: they receive only a passing reference in his next work, the *Focus of Life*, and none in *The Anathema of Zos* (apart from the title!). It is suggested that he abandoned them because he saw that they were becoming a system, and he was against systematisation. I think that the evidence is that Spare was quite clearly building a philosophy or 'personal religion' in *Earth Inferno* and *The Book of Pleasure*. He ceased adding to it at that point for the following reasons:

a. he'd finished it;
b. he wanted to just 'live it' – 'now, not eventually';
c. he'd presented it to Aleister Crowley for an endorsement, which, to his disappointment, had not been forthcoming;
d. life was keeping him busy by jumping up and kicking him in the teeth.

Perhaps the completion of the *Book of Pleasure* also marked the end of Spare's youthful idealism. Following publication of the *Anathema of Zos*, Spare broke with the respectable art world, moved south of the river, and entered a distinctly 'low' period of his life. This period has been presented by Grant as a kind of voluntary Buddhistic retreat into stoical contemplation, but while I accept that this is what it may have become, I think it likely to have been triggered by some more tangible catastrophic event in Spare's life. While it is tempting to speculate upon what this may have been, the recent failure of his marriage was probably enough.

It has been objected that Spare's main message is in his art, not his texts. Whilst this may be true, it is still evident that Spare put a lot of effort into his writings, and that they were meant to work alongside his art: for this reason, too, I encourage the reader to return to the original in facsimile form, and see the illustrations that are such an important part of The *Book of Pleasure*.

Some have already objected to what they regard as the 'demystification' of Spare. To them I would respond that this is far from being my intention, which is merely to make the philosophy he worked so hard on accessible to a wider audience. As the reader will see, there is still many a mysterious conundrum to ponder: Spare's ideas, even when expressed in the plainest possible language, are still highly abstruse. Some who have seen early drafts of my work have complained that it could have done with being in yet plainer English! The *Book of Pleasure* will never be an easy book to read, but I like to think that I may at least have helped transform a book that was nearly impossible to comprehend into one that is merely difficult.

C. J. CHIBNALL, 2014

Introduction

Look up into the sky. Just at the limits of the outer atmosphere begins a region known to us as 'space,' and for a very good reason; because it consists of precisely that – an inconceivably and infinitely vast panorama, with virtually nothing at all in it. The stars, the planets, and even very minor planetary moons, are, it is true, enormous when seen up close; yet viewed from outside the cosmic arena they might as well not be there at all. The total mass of matter floating around out there is dwarfed into mere speckdom by the amount of sheer empty *space* around, above, beyond and in between it.

Let us invert our vision and peer down into the atom, the microcosmic substance; what, if anything, can we find down there? Well, according to post-

Einsteinian physics, a great deal more nothingness actually – vast expanses of the stuff, alleviated but rarely by a glimpse of one of the sparse itinerant population of particles, many of which hove into and out of existence for the briefest imaginable span of time, and most of which are entirely fictitious, or perhaps we may say 'theoretical'. Nothing and nobody much there but an emptiness as deep and abiding as the interstellar wastelands above our heads.

Pound for pound, then, there is infinitely more nothingness than somethingness in the universe; existence – the so-called 'real', or 'reality' to which we cling – appears to be no more than a flimsy, motley raiment, hung on an armature of absence and wafting gently in the stellar breeze. Viewed in this light, Death – non-being – is the normal state of being, and Life a rare activity carried on only in the tiniest corners of a vast nowhere – a desperate, perpetually doomed attempt to paper over the abyssal gaps of limitless and eternal nullity.

Enter at this point the artist-mage Austin Osman Spare, who attained this realization early on in his creative career, wearing a disconcertingly mischievous grin and carrying something partly-concealed behind his back; his secret weapon – the *Book of Pleasure*.

The intrinsic non-existence at the heart of entity is what Spare designated the *Kiā*, and he strove to convey his vision in a theory enshrined as the very keystone of the *Book of Pleasure*. To this, he wedded a new and radical model of transcendental sorcery that completely rejected all religious ethos and utilised instead those techniques that were most familiar to him, and most fully within his mastery as an artist and designer: for its language, line and letter synthesized as the Sigil and the Sacred Alphabet; for its praxis, the sense of sight extended through touch, emotion and profound nostalgia into a willed and magically fecund synaesthesia that attains its apotheosis in the Death Posture.

The *Book of Pleasure* was a radical departure for magic when it was published in 1913, in its refusal to advance a new dispensation or 'doctrine' (as Crowley had done) – indeed, in its intent to overcome the bonds imposed upon raw sorcery by traditional religious thinking. Its concepts remain as radical today, whether applied in a strictly magical or psychological context. Why, then, did Spare's ideas fail to gain any currency until around sixty years after his exposition? Was it purely because the work itself remained inaccessible until the books of Kenneth and Steffi Grant, and later Francis King and Neville Drury, brought them into wider circulation? In part, yes, but that is not the sole reason. Even given the masterly expositions of Spare's creed from these authors, the work itself is yet little understood or applied.

I think the main obstacle to a wide appreciation of the value of Spare's work has remained the fact that the *Book of Pleasure* makes for rather difficult reading. In large part this is due to Spare's habit of writing beyond the means of his educational economy. Spare himself coyly acknowledged this shortcoming; to a manuscript page from *Logomachy* written in the early 1950s in which he reflected critically on magic in the modern age, Spare added the note: 'As an illiterate youth I formulated a simple thesis; see 'Book of Pleasure''. Further, the book was collated and published under pressure of both time and money, and did not benefit from the attentions of an editor. A comparison of its prose with that of *The Focus of Life* (1921), edited by his friend and co-editor of *Form* magazine Frederick Carter, shows how the *Book of Pleasure* might have appeared had its many obvious grammatical and other errors been corrected. Conceptually and linguistically, *The Focus of Life* is no less challenging than the *Book of Pleasure*, but the harsher edges of Spare's style were evidently smoothed off and the division of the volume into a collation of aphorisms, followed by a sequence of short episodic narrative chapters, makes it a much more manageable prospect. Of course, apart from the support of Carter, Spare's ability as a writer had by that time matured, and he had found useful models in earlier prose stylists including the impassioned cadences of Nietzsche's *Also sprach Zarathustra*.

So there's no need to get upset over my proposal that the *Book of Pleasure* is less than well-written, and that this factor – as much as its mystical import – accounts for its apparent impenetrability. You've thought it yourself, and that is one reason you are holding this book. Somewhat paradoxically, this aspect of the *Book of Pleasure* is a vital part of its alluring mystique. How many times have we read and re-read a passage of the book, knowing that there is a perfectly rational sense hid within it that refuses to yield to the grasp of our rational comprehension? Or thumbed through the book in search of a fondly-remembered quote without being able to find it – as if the contents quietly re-assemble themselves between the covers while the book sits, feigning innocence, upon the shelf. For many, myself included, the linguistic and grammatical faults of the book are part of its attraction – they help to create the tone that is so uniquely 'Sparean', and if the greatness of a writer can be gauged by how easily they can be identified from just a short, randomly chosen passage of their work, then Spare certainly qualifies as a great writer. With Spare's vitality of expression his text – wedded to the cryptic drawings in black-and-white and the seething, effulgent page illustrations – ensures that *The Book of Pleasure*, as a grimoire of magic, can claim the rare distinction of being quite literally magical and evocative in and of itself.

Years ago, I heard it said – by an admirer and student of the mage – that although Spare had been translated into German, he had not been translated into English. It was a telling observation and one that I did not ever expect to be rebutted. Yet Mr. Chibnall, himself an artist of distinction as well as magician and therapeutic psychologist, decided to take the courageous, probably controversial and to some foolhardy step of interpreting Spare's text methodically and sympathetically, in order to render it in plain and consistent English. The book he has produced is an admirable and, I feel, essential companion to one of the greatest occult texts of the modern era; you will enjoy it immensely and will find new insights into *The Book of Pleasure*, and I hope – for Spare's sake! – that you will also find plenty of points of disagreement. One of the unique virtues of the *Book of Pleasure* is that it critiques not only the content of magical theory and practice but also their form, demanding a constant interrogation and revaluation of the Art – by the methods of art. Not only is Spare's work still appreciated eighty years after its publication, but it continues to stimulate creative debate among practitioners, a process that will undoubtedly be enriched and informed by the book you are about to read.

GAVIN W. SEMPLE

CHAPTER I

Definitions

The words God, religion, faith, morals, woman, etc., are abstract nouns and are to be considered as expressions of belief, rather than as things in themselves. As such, they are used as different 'means' of controlling and expressing desire. They can be used in this way to express an idea of longed-for unity, eg. with 'God', 'woman', or the rest of 'humankind'. However, they do this by means of fear in some form or other, which ultimately entails bondage to imagined limits.

Science [a relatively new addition to this list] although it may at first appear to promise freedom, ultimately leads to its own form of bondage and limits; it can be said to have added a dearly-paid inch to our height: no more.

Kiã

Kiã is absolute freedom: it is that from which ever-changing 'reality' comes, but since it is itself free from change or limitation, it is ultimately the only reality.

It is free at any time, and is therefore not made manifest, or even potential, by mere ideas of freedom or 'means' such as those listed above, but by the Ego becoming free to receive it, by being free from ideas about it and by not 'believing'.

The less said of Kiã, the fewer untruths will be said about it, and the less obscure it will be. Remember that evolution teaches – and by terrible punishments – that conception creates what we call 'reality' but is not freedom from evolution, since things and ideas that are conceived are subject to change, and never permanent.

Virtue

Pure Art: (i.e. the freedom to create for pleasure or interest).[1]

Vice

Fear, belief, control, science, and the like: all these are antithetical to freedom.

Self-Love

A mental state, mood, or condition in which the Ego is able to unite with Kiā before entering the realm of conception and limitation: the emotion of laughter is the principle that allows this.

Exhaustion

That state of vacuity brought about by exhausting a desire by some means of dissipation at times of disappointment, i.e. when the mind is worried because of the non-fulfilment of a desire and seeks relief. Seizing the moment, and utilizing the emotional energy that would otherwise have been expended in the anticipated activity, results in a vacuity that is sensitive to the suggestions carried by a Sigil [see later].

CHAPTER 2

Different Religions and Doctrines as Means to Pleasure, Freedom and Power

What is there to believe, but in Self? We, as limited Egos, can never see the complete Self in limited so-called 'reality', as it is both literally and potentially boundless. No man has seen Self at any time.

We are what we believe – and what our beliefs imply: these implications are worked out in a process of conception over time. Creation is caused by this bondage to the formula of what we believe, both consciously and unconsciously. Actions are the expressions of ideas that are bound up in beliefs. These ideas [or unconscious beliefs] are inherent and their operation indirect, so they are obscure and easily escape introspection.

It has been said that the fruits of action may be two-fold; either Heaven or Hell.[2]

To these states can be added Purgatory and Indifference, so we have:

a. Heaven, where there is desire [e.g.] for women.
b. Hell, where that desire is more intense, to the point of pain.
c. Purgatory – where Heaven and Hell are united, in the form of expectation delayed.
d. Indifference – nothingness, neither Heaven nor Hell. It is the state of disappointment until the original desire recovers.

Then surely, Heaven and Hell are one and the same. The wise pleasure-seeker, having realised they are but different 'degrees' of desire, gives up both Virtue and Vice and becomes a Kiā-ist. Riding the Shark of his desire, he crosses the ocean of the Dual Principle[3] and engages himself in self-love.

Religions are but projections resulting from incapacity, and imaginings resulting from fear. They are a superficially attractive veneer over the superstition that paradox is 'truth' (e.g. in the case of Christianity, the paradox that God is always in Heaven, or that the Almighty inconceivable emanates its conception or negation, or that the Almighty – in the form of Christ – commits suicide, etc.).

Religion is just an ornament upon imbecility. For example, certain people have the idea that to maximise pleasure cheaply, you can have your 'sins' pardoned and excused… but this whole system is just a puppet-show, an expression of the governing fear. Yes! What you people have decreed in your religiousness is just a rack you have created for yourself, even if it is only imaginary! Your prospects are not pleasant… it is deeply ingrained into your unconscious that these imaginary sins will hurt you, and your body is sensitive.[4]

Some praise the idea of faith: they think that believing they are gods (or anything else) will make them such. But they merely prove, by all that they do, that they do not really believe it. It is better to admit incapacity or insignificance than to reinforce it by faith. Conscious belief is superficial, and 'protects' – but does not change – the vital.

Therefore, reject expressed belief – and exchange it for the possibility of genuine change. The believers' formula is a deception and they are deceived – which is a negation of their purpose. Faith is denial, and the metaphor for faith is idiocy, hence it always fails. To make their power more secure, governments force religion down the throats of their slaves, and it always succeeds. Few people escape it; therefore the honour of those who do is all the greater. When faith perishes, the 'Self' comes into its own.

Others, less foolish, deliberately obscure the memory that God is a conception of themselves, and just as much subject to law. So is this ambition to have a lot of faith really so very desirable? Myself, I have not yet seen anyone who is not God already.

Others again, though they have much knowledge, cannot tell you exactly what 'belief' is, or how to believe in what defies natural laws and existing beliefs. Surely one cannot do it by saying 'I believe': that art has long been lost. They become even more subject to bewilderment and distraction as soon as they open their own mouths, which are full of argument: they feel powerless and unhappy unless they are engaged in spreading their own confusion. To appear cogent, they must adopt dogma and mannerisms that appear to exclude any possibility of doubt or ambiguity.

As they appear to increase their knowledge, their attainment actually decreases: they decay in ratio to their expounding. A human being can neither believe by faith nor gain in knowledge through it: neither can they explain their knowledge unless it; is born of a new law. If we already are everything, why do we need to imagine we are not?

Be Ye Mystic

Others believe in prayer... but haven't they yet learned that to ask is to be denied? Let that be the root of your Gospel. Oh, you who are living other people's lives!

Unless desire is unconscious, it is not fulfilled, no, not in this life. Then surely, sleep is better than prayer. Quiescence is hidden desire; a form of 'not asking', and by it, the female obtains much from the male.[5] Utilize prayer (if you must pray) as a means to exhaustion, and by that you will obtain your desire.

Some try to show the similarities between different religions: I think that rather, they show evidence of a fundamental and universal illusion. Such people fail to realise that they themselves are a mockery of this arbitrary edict – perhaps because they have much to regret! They suffer more conflict than the 'unenlightened', and whatever they can identify with their own delusion of fear they call truth. In emphasising these apparent similarities between religions, they cover up the real truth, in a way that reflects their own poverty of imagination. It would be better to show the essential differences between different religions: then it could be seen that what they have in common is their various means: is it not their object to deceive and govern?[6] Surely, then, for the attainment of the transcendent, God and religion should have no place.

Some praise so-called 'truth' but give it many containers. They go out to 'prove' its relativity and paradoxical nature, from their experience and disillusionment.

However, they forget its dependent nature: paradox is not a central 'Truth' but the truth that anything can be true for a time. Paradox implies a 'not necessary': what supersedes both paradox and this 'not necessary' I will make the foundation of my teaching. Let us first determine the arena of debate: the 'truth' cannot be divided, but is a continuum. Only self-love cannot be divided: it remains such when paradoxical and under any condition; hence, it alone is truth and complete without anything else.[7]

Some praise ceremonial Magic, and are supposed to suffer much Ecstasy! Our asylums are crowded, the stage is over-run! Is it by symbolizing we become the symbolized? If I were to crown myself King, should I be King? Rather should I be an object of disgust or pity? These Magicians, whose insincerity is their safety, are but the unemployed dandies of the Brothels. Magic is but one's natural ability to attract without asking; ceremony what is unaffected, its doctrine the negation of theirs. I know them well and their creed of learning that teaches the fear of their own light. Vampires, they are the very lice in attraction. Their practices prove their incapacity; they have no magic to intensify the normal, the joy of a child or healthy person, none to evoke their pleasure or wisdom from themselves. Their methods depending on a morass of the imagination and a chaos of conditions, their knowledge obtained with less decency than a hyena his food, they are less free and do not obtain the satisfaction of the meanest among animals. Self condemned in their disgusting fatness, their emptiness of power, without even the magic of personal charm or beauty, they are offensive in their bad taste and mongering for advertisement. The freedom of energy is not obtained by putting it in bondage, great power not by disintegration. Is it not because our energy (or mind stuff) is already over bound and divided, that we are not capable, let alone magical?[8]

Some believe that any and everything is symbolic, and can be transcribed and used to explain the occult, but symbolic of what they do not know (great spiritual truths, perhaps?). So they argue by means of metaphor, cautiously confusing the obvious in a way they think develops some hidden virtue. This unnecessary fatness by the accretion of collected 'symbols', however impressive, is it not also disgusting? (The elephant is exceedingly large, but unlike them, also exceedingly powerful; the swine may smell bad, but unlike them, does not breed the contempt of our good taste). If a man is no hero to his servant, can he remain a mystic to the eyes of the curious? They will sense that he is not so much different from them, and from there it is but a small step to feeling able to mimic him.

Embellish your meaning, however objectionable it may be as fact, only after you have demonstrated your honesty. The truth, though simple, never needs be made confused or obscure: symbolism embraces all possibilities as mystic design. Take your stand in common sense and you include the truth that cannot lie: no argument against it has yet prevailed. These 'symbolists' reject the idea that anything modern can be symbolic, and reach an absurd limit as to what can be regarded as 'symbolic' very early on. It is important to realise that modern means of locomotion, machinery, government, institutions, etc., may be vital symbols of the workings of the modern mind.

These people fail to count on change, and the (at times) arbitrary nature of symbolism, or the possibility of a preserved folly. For example, the symbol of Justice known to the Romans is not necessarily symbolic either of divine justice or our justice.

To take another example, the vitality is not always exactly like water, which is sometimes used to symbolise it. Similarly, although our natures may be symbolised by a Tree, we are not trees:[9] we are ourselves (which may include trees somewhere unheard), and that we are ourselves is much more obvious than our being trees in our workings at present. By assuming that traditional symbols are directly applicable to the present, these people try to work with a symbolism that is actually chaotic and meaningless. Not really knowing the original meaning of ancient symbols, they are more successful in projecting their own meagreness onto them than they are in explaining them. This conglomeration of decayed antiquity, collected with the disease of greed, surely invites our charity. It would be better to forget these trumpery ideas, and learn the best of traditions by observing your own functions, and regarding modernity in an unbiased way.[10]

Some praise the belief in a moral doctrinal code, which they naturally and continually transgress, and they never obtain their purpose. Given the right nature, nevertheless, they succeed fairly well in governing themselves, and of all the types of people I have listed, they can be among the most healthy, sane and self-pleased.

However, this may be called the negation of my doctrine, for although they may obtain tolerable satisfaction, my doctrine offers complete satisfaction. Let him remain here, who is not strong enough for the great work, otherwise he might find himself lost in freedom. But fledge your wings fearlessly, ye humble ones!

Others say that only knowledge is eternal, but knowledge is really just the eternal illusion of re-learning what we already know. As soon as we ask ourselves 'how', we induce stupidity. Without this conception, what is there we could not know and accomplish?

Yet others swear by 'concentration'. However, concentration will not free you, because the mind conceiving the law is bondage; having arrived at that, you will want de-concentration! Dissociation from all ideas but one is not release but imaginative fulfilment, or the fury of creation.

Others again believe that all things are emanations of the divine spirit, like rays of the sun – does it follow that we need release and liberation? Verily, things only become necessary as a result of their conception and belief. So let us destroy or change conception, and empty the belief [of content].

These and many other doctrines are declared by me as the perpetuators of restriction and illusion. Each and all of these doctrines depend on a muddled implication, obscuring, yet evolved from, the duality of the consciousness.

If their followers could see the fruit of their actions and pleasures, they would vomit hot blood in their fear. Although these people believe in wildly different doctrines, their philosophies all fall under the dual principle, and are necessary parasites on each other. Like drugs and the surgeon's knife, they only alleviate, or at best remove, a symptom. They do not change or remove the fundamental cause (the law).[11]

"Oh God, thou art the stagnant environment'.[12] All is quackery: these religions, whose very existence depends on their failure, are full of misery and confusion.

They have only multiplied arguments, and are as full of argument as they are evil. They are crowded with non-essentials, yet are so barren of any free pleasure in either this life or another, that I cannot uphold their doctrine. Their criterion for enjoyment is death! It would be better for a man to renounce them all, and embrace his own invincible purpose. He cannot go any further than that, and this is his only real release. By it he may put his pleasure where he will, and find satisfaction.

CHAPTER 3

The Consumer
of Religion

Kiã, in its Transcendental and Conceivable Manifestation

I t really has no name to designate it. I call it Kiã, and dare not claim it as myself.

The Kiã that can be expressed as conceivable ideas is not the eternal Kiã, but the archetype of 'Self', the slavery of mortality, whereas the Eternal Kiã burns up all belief.[13] All conception is by the dual principle, a law that also applies to the conception of this 'Self'. By endeavouring to describe it, I am in danger of writing what may be – but not usually – called the 'book of lies' about it.[14]

I here present an unorthodox view of ultimate origins, taking a 'bird's eye view', and hoping to convey somehow by the incidental, that the truth is somewhere.

The Kiã that can be vaguely expressed in words is the 'Neither-Neither', the unmodified 'I' that manifests in a feeling of omnipresence. Its illumination is symbolically transcribed in the sacred alphabet of which I am about to write.

It emanates its own intensity, but is necessary only to itself, for it always has, and always will, exist: it is the irreducible, virgin quantum, and by its exuberance we have gained existence. Who dare say where, why, how and to what it is related?

By his labour over time, the doubter inhabits his limited existence. It is not related to anything, but permits everything. It eludes any attempt at conception, but is itself the quintessence of conception, and through it we find pleasure in meaning.

It comes before Heaven and Earth, and in as much as it transcends these, it may be regarded as the primordial sexual principle, the idea of pleasure in self-love.

Only he who has attained the Death Posture can apprehend this new sexuality, and the satisfaction of its almighty love. He who is forever the servant of belief, and clogged with unsatisfied desire, is identified with the belief and can only see its infinite ramifications in dissatisfaction.[15] The unmodified sex principle refracted through the dual principle emanates the wide variety of emotions or sexualities, which may be called its ramifications.

This sexuality is the progenitor of itself and all things, but itself resembles nothing, and in its original simplicity it embodies the everlasting. Time has not changed it, hence I call it 'new'. This ancestral sexual principle, and the idea of self, are one and the same. In this identity with the self lies its demand and its infinite possibilities, the earliest duality, the mystery of mysteries, the Sphinx at the gates of all spirituality. All conceivable ideas begin and end in the light of its emotion, the ecstasy which the creation of the idea of self induces. This idea is that of unity by the formula of self, and its reality becomes necessary as a matter of continuity. The question of the existence of all things, and the whole of the universe, visible and invisible, has come out of it. As unity conceived duality, it begot trinity, begot Tetragrammaton.[16]

Because Duality is Unity, it is also identical with time; the whole complex unfolding of conception is implied in it, and it represents the eternal cycle of return to the primeval reality that is freedom. Included in it, the six senses represent a trinity of dualities: also included in it are the five facets of sex.[17] Through these aspects of existence, the human environment or 'reality' is projected in a process of self-assimilation, which involves a denial that 'outside reality' is formed from aspects of one's self, in a process of complete sexuality.

The complex of information that is humanity can be represented by a Tetragrammaton of dualities that is twelve-fold by arrangement, and may be called the twelve commandments of the believer.[18] Unity imagines the eternal decimal, its multiplicity embracing the whole of eternity, from which spring the manifold forms, which constitute existence. Vitalized by the breath of self-love, life is conscious of one. Self being unity's opposing force, there is alternately conflict and harmony, life and death. These four principles are one and the same – the whole conception considered as the complete 'self' or consciousness – hence they may be blended into unity and symbolized as one form made by two, that is three-fold and having four directions.[19]

The Transcendental Law, The Law and Testament of the 'New'

The law of Kiā is its own judge, beyond force or compulsion: who can grasp the nameless Kiā? It is obvious but unintelligible, without form, but excellently designed.

What it wishes for is its own superabundance, so who can assert its mysterious purpose? The more we try to know about it, the more obscure and remote it becomes, and by our trying to have faith in it, we just make it more opaque. It has no attributes, and I don't know its name. How free it is – it has no need of sovereignty! (Remember that kingdoms are their own despoilers).[20] Without lineage, who dare claim relationship to it? Without virtue, how pleasing is its moral self-love!

Self-love, in its proper perspective, serves its own invincible purpose of ecstasy: it is balanced by a supreme bliss that simulates opposition. It suffers no hurt, neither does it labour. Is it not self-attracting and independent? Assuredly we could not call it balance. If we could imitate its law, all creation without command would unite and serve our purpose in pleasure and harmony. As Kiā transcends conception, it is unchanging and inexhaustible – hence there is no need of illumination to see it.

If we open our mouths to speak of it, we speak not of it but only of our own duality, mighty though that may be in its primordial simplicity! Kiā, without conceiving, produces its meeting-point as the fullness of creation. Although without assertion it is the mightiest energy, and although without smallness it is the least among things, we can have it without asking, because being free it is the only thing that is truly free.

Without distinguishing characteristics, it has no preferences, but sustains itself. Out of fear, all creation pays homage to it, but does not praise it in terms of right or wrong so that everything in creation, when it eventually perishes, does so unbeautifully and without sentimental meaning. We endow ourselves with the power we conceive from it and it acts as our master, never as a cause of liberation. In what way can it act as master? Through scores of incarnations, the 'self' we end up with is derived from the attributes with which we endow our God, the abstract Ego or conceptive principles. All conception is a denial of the Kiā, and hence we human beings are its opposition, our own evil. As we are the offspring of ourselves, we are the conflict between whatever we deny and assert of the Kiā. It would seem that we cannot be too careful in our choice, for it determines the body we inhabit.

Thus forever from 'self' do I fashion the Kiā, which may be without likeness, but which may be regarded as the truth. From this process is the bondage made, and not through intellect shall we be free from it. The law of Kiā is always its own original purpose, undetermined by anything else, and its emanations are unchanging.

Through our own conceptive process things materialize, and take their nature from that duality. Human beings take their law from this refraction, and their ideas create their reality. With what do they balance their ecstasy? They pay measure for measure with intense pain, sorrow, and miseries. With what do they balance their rebellion? Of necessity, with slavery!

Duality is the law, and realization by experience relates and opposes by units of time. Ecstasy for any length of time is difficult to obtain, and takes a lot of work.

The conditions of consciousness and existence would seem to be various degrees of misery alternating with gusts of pleasure and some more subtle emotions.

Consciousness of existence consists of duality in some form or other. From it are created the illusions of time, size, entity, etc.: the world's limit.

The dual principle is the quintessence of all experience, and no ramification has enlarged its primordial simplicity, but can only be its repetition, modification or complexity: its evolution can never be complete. It can never go further than the experience of self, so returns and unites again and again, ever an anti-climax.

Its evolution consists of forever returning to its original simplicity by infinite complication. No man shall understand its 'reason why' by looking at its workings.

Know it as the illusion that embraces the learning of all existence. It is the most aged one who grows no wiser, and is the mother of all things. Therefore believe all 'experience' to be an illusion, and the result of the law of duality. Just as space pervades an object both inside and outside it, similarly within and beyond this ever-changing cosmos, there is this single principle.

CHAPTER 4

Soliloquy on God-Head

Whoever Thought Thus?

Something is causing Pain and energises the Agony: may this cause not be the latent idea of Supreme Bliss? And this eternal expectation, this amassing of ornament upon something that is decaying, this ever-abiding thought: could this have something to do with the vanity that precedes death? What a squalid, morbid, depressing thought – I asked it, 'how can I accept you, yet save my soul'? Ever did it answer back, 'pay homage where it's due: the Physician is the Lord of Existence!' Medicine is just another variety of superstition: is it not the essence of cowardice, the agent of Death?[21]

Isn't it strange that no-one remembers being dead? Have you ever seen the Sun? If you have then you have seen nothing 'dead' – despite you believing differently! Which is the more dead – 'you' or this corpse? Which of you has the greater degree of consciousness? Judging by the expression alone, which of you appears to be enjoying life most? May not this 'belief' in a state of death be the 'will' that attempts that state for your satisfaction, but can give you no more than sleep, decay, change- hell? This constant sleep-walking is 'the unsatisfactory'.[22]

So you disbelieve in Ghosts and God- because you 'have not seen them'? What! Haven't you seen the mocking ghosts of your beliefs- the Laughing Bedlam of your 'humility', or Mammon, or your grotesque ideas of 'Self'? Yes, your very faculties and most courageous lies are Gods! Who is the slayer of your Gods – but a God! You say there is no proof that you have existed before? What an excuse! You say that no-one has returned to tell us? What a damning plea!

Are you but what you were – somehow changed? Are you the case at first sight that you are reincarnated to perhaps anything? 'Perhapses' are possibilities!

Can you do any differently to what you do? I shall never tire of asserting that you constantly do differently! What is the 'ugliness' that offends? Is it the vague knowledge that one day you will have to change your mind or that you are germinating what you contain? You are always remembering what you forgot – but might today be the day of reckoning, the day you are forced to believe what you once disbelieved? Now if today is just yesterday in all but appearances, then tomorrow is also today, the day of decay! Every day this universe is destroyed, that is why you are conscious! Is there no Life and Death? Such ideas should be less than comic.[23]

There is no Duality?

You are conscious of the gay butterfly you observe and are conscious of being 'you'. However, the butterfly is conscious of being itself, and, as such, it has a consciousness as good as and the same as yours. So could this consciousness of 'you' that you both feel be the same 'you'? Therefore, you are one and the same – the mystery of mysteries and the easiest thing in the world to understand![24]

So, if you hurt the butterfly you hurt yourself, but your belief that you don't hurt yourself protects you from hurt – for a time! Belief, though, eventually becomes exhausted and you are miserably hurt! Do what you will – belief is ever its own inconsistency. Desire contains everything– hence you must believe in everything, if you believe at all!

Belief seems to exclude common sense. This consciousness of 'thee' and 'me' constantly torments us – but does not need to! Perhaps you are afraid of entering a den of tigers (and I assure you it is a matter of righteousness whether you go voluntarily or are chucked in, and whether you come out alive or not!), yet daily you enter dens inhabited by more terrible creatures than tigers [i.e. human beings] and you come out unharmed – why?

The Allegory

Great scientists are uncovering the death-dealing properties of the microbes they discover that we breathe, and which according to them we should destroy. So why aren't we dead already? Have faith! The teachings of science are quite correct, and do not disappoint our doubts. Our greater familiarity with them will certainly bring us the disease and death they give! And will also give us in compensation their powers of destruction! But for the destruction of whom? Things will be put straight! Is this the value of the will? This 'will to power' – how life-preserving! How furthering of discriminate selection! How pleasing! What noble explorers you scientists are – go on discovering the bottomless pit! When you are sodden with science, will the lightning thunder out the murder? Will new hope be born? Will there be new creatures for the circus?

The conception of being a God can only be maintained by a continual process of evolution, otherwise it is in constant danger of changing to its very opposite, which God hood itself contains. Must the master be the painful learner of his own stupidity? The idea of God hood constantly requires the forgetting of its own supremacy and Godliness, so it must be supplanted by fear, eh? Is there really no true Atheist, no-one free from his own past, no fearless pleasurist?

Any conception is only the absence of its own indisputable inner reality. When the conception is remembered together with its own opposite, may this be your chance to see its real nature? When the prayer (you are always praying) has been transmuted into its corresponding blasphemous opposite, only then are you attractive enough to be heard, and your desire gratified! What a somersault of humility! Whether God is projected as an external master by means of fear or as a dweller within by means of love, we are Gods all the time – that is why 'divinity' is always potential. It constantly generates eternal delay- which is life. This envy of the Master or Creator, and ultimate hope to follow in like manner, is also a way of merely existing and forfeiting 'Life'. There is no scientific 'fact', because it always implies its opposite as equal fact: that's the real 'fact'! Then why bother to prove anything as a fact?

This vain hope to prove finality is death itself, a waste of time and energy, so why cheat the 'Desire'? You have proven by means of mathematics that the sun is so many millions more miles away than previously thought, but you have had to make it more powerful, to account for the heat we still receive from it. Nature – that constant, living impulse to be the antithesis of your 'truth' will soon prove – again by mathematics, or whatever you like – that the sun does not exist at all! Or (if you wish) it will prove conclusively that the Sun is millions of millions of miles further away or millions and millions of miles nearer than you thought! What an extraordinary thinker you are![25] These facts and many others are already known to the butterfly, the lice, the insects and – perhaps, intuitively – yourself? Whose senses are the truest: yours, or the house-flies'? You will eventually adopt their vision

– their thoughts and wisdom – were you such once? You are such now, but have not yet awakened these attributes: you will be such again in power![26] Now there's real progress! Conveniently, science can be used to study both your progress and what you have gained by it. You are always what you most wish.[27]

Your desire is always to live according to your desire: which is just what you are always doing anyway! 'Consciousness' is the only illusion: this consciousness can be thought of as a kind of monument to commemorate whether or not you have really enjoyed life! The God of 'The Will' is actually the command to obey.[28]

Everyone fears the sword of its 'justice'- which is what you deserve for obedience to it! 'Will' is also the command to believe. Your 'Will' is what you have believed, actively willing the belief for you! You think only when 'it', the 'will' wishes! Will is not an end, it is the means of a means- thus it is just a complication.

Whether you call this 'Will' free or not, beyond Will and Belief is Self-Love. Self-love is free to believe what it desires. You are free to believe in nothing related to belief. The 'Truth' is not difficult to understand: the Truth has no will, and will no truth! The truth is that 'will' has never believed.

'Could be' is the only immediate thing we can say with certainty. Does this haunting Sphinx teach us the value of the 'will to...' anything? Then there can be no greater risk than 'absolute Knowledge': if only a little knowledge of it is dangerous, then what about Omniscience? There is nothing one can add to an already mighty power!

Science is the accursed doubt directed at all that is possible, or indeed that exists! You cannot conceive impossibility: nothing is truly impossible, indeed you are the impossible! Doubt is only delay – but how it punishes! Nothing is truer than anything else. What are you not? Have you ever answered this truthfully?

You tyrannise over yourself, so constantly forget what you remember: you resist sense objects and your faculties of perceiving them by your either believing or not believing. These faculties are as numerous as the atoms you have not seen, and as endless as the number one: they come into life at will. You adopt a few at a time, you speak knowledge through them, and if you did but understand your grammar then those you disown would speak louder than your words! I would not believe the wisdom of the Almighty.

Belief is ever its own tempter to believe differently. You cannot believe freedom into existence, but can you free yourself from belief? You cannot believe the 'Truth' into existence either, but you need not compromise yourself. The Way of Life is not by 'means', not even of my own doctrines, though they may allow the self-appointed to emulate my own realisation – may I never cease to be embarrassed by this! How ironic it is that the Man of Sorrows is here the teacher! I have taught – would I choose to teach myself or yourself again? No – not even for a gift from heaven! Mastership equals learning and constant unlearning! Almighty is he who has not learned – and Almighty also is the baby, who only assimilates!

The most uncouth of fools now asks: 'But how can we escape the inevitable evolutions of conception, since all is forever conceiving?' My answer is true for all situations: listen, you who are God already, yet still want to be God. When the mind is confused to the point that it comes to a standstill, it is then that the capability of attempting the apparently impossible becomes known: by that simple state of 'Neither-Neither' the Ego becomes the 'Silent Watcher' or 'Observer' and understands it all![29] The 'Why' and 'How' of desire are contained within the mystic state of 'Neither-Neither', and it is such a source of nutrition to life that it may be called the 'milk state'. Although I am but a clownish fool, all my ideas and yours have come out of it, and although I myself am lazy, regard me as an old sinner who would see others exalted before himself.

CHAPTER 5

The Death Posture

I deas about the 'self' conflict with each other and cannot be slain – their very resistance is what gives them the appearance of reality. Neither death nor cunning can overcome them, but only reinforce their energy. The dead are reborn again, and find themselves lying in the womb of conscience. To allow full development is to assert decay. On the other hand, non-resistance to these ideas represents a regression to primordial simplicity, and to the original unity, uncontaminated by 'ideas'.

In this way, non-resistance to these ideas creates the state of 'does not matter – please yourself'. The conception 'I am not' necessarily follows "I am" as surely as night follows day. The idea of pain implies the idea of pleasure, and so it is with all ideas. By means of this duality, remember to laugh at all times, recognise all things, resist nothing, and there will then be no conflict, incompatibility or compulsion.[30]

Transgressing Conception by a Lucid Symbolism

Man implies Woman: these can be transcended by the concept of the hermaphrodite (having both sexes): this again implies the eunuch (having no sex), and all these conditions I transcend yet again by another 'Neither' principle: yet although this 'Neither' is vague, it is perceivable by the mind, and again implies yet another 'Neither', and so on.

These abstract dualities have an analogy with certain primordial sex principles in nature.[31] They are carried further in the Sacred Alphabet, being too abstruse to explain by orthodox words and grammar. The 'Neither-Neither' principle is the state in which the mind has passed beyond conception, and cannot be balanced with anything else, since it implies only itself. The 'I' principle has reached the 'does not matter, need not be' state, and is not related to form. There is nothing but it, and nothing beyond it, so therefore it alone is complete and eternal. It is indestructible itself, but has the power to destroy – therefore it alone is true freedom and existence. Through it comes immunity from all sorrow: therefore its spirit is ecstasy. Renounce everything by the Neither-Neither meditation, and take shelter in the Neither-Neither state. Surely it is the abode of the Kiā? It is our unconditional release from duality and time: it is effective even if only symbolically reached. Once the belief is free from all ideas except pleasure, the Karma of displeasure speedily exhausts itself through Karmic law. In that moment beyond time, the ego becomes its own gratifier by its own law, its every wish gratified without the payment of sorrow. Here, there is no necessitation; 'does not matter-need not be' and 'please your self' are its creeds. In that state, what you wish to believe can be true, without subjection to beliefs from outside. The Ego has now become the Absolute, and can be pleased by this imitation of the means of government: he uses these means, but is himself ungoverned. Kiā is the supreme bliss; this is the psychology of ecstasy by non-resistance.

The Ritual and Doctrine

So here is the method for the Death Posture. Gaze at your reflection in a mirror until it becomes blurred and you know not the gazer. Close your eyes and visualise.[32] You will see a light in the form of an 'X' in curious evolutions. Hold on to this until doing so is no longer an effort. You will, within this small form, gain a feeling of immensity whose limit you will never reach.[33]

Practice these steps before moving on to trying the next stage: the emotion that is felt is the knowledge that tells you why. Next, stand on tiptoe with the arms rigid, hands clasped behind you, and, straining to the utmost, with the neck stretched, breathe deeply and spasmodically until you are giddy and sensation comes in gusts.[34]

Now lie down quickly on your back and relax, the body expressing the condition of yawning, suspiring while conceiving by smiling. Forget about time, together with all those things that once seemed essential: they have now become meaningless. This moment is beyond time, and its virtue has already happened.[35]

The Death Posture is its own inevitability accelerated, and through it we escape our own unending delay that is caused by attachment. The Ego is swept up like a leaf in a gale, and in the swiftness of the indeterminable, that which is always about to happen becomes truth to the Ego. Things that were obscure now become self-evident, as the Ego pleases itself by its own will. This is the end of the duality of the consciousness: it is the negation of all faith by simply living. In place of belief is a positive death state, and all that remains of belief is sleep, a negative state. This sleep is the dead body of all we believe. The Ego, which was previously subjected to law, now seeks stillness in sleep and death. The Death Posture and its alternative reality represent freedom from law, and ascension from duality. In the final cataclysm, the universe may be reduced to ashes, and no-one will be sorry, but the Ego will escape the Judgement! In that final freedom there is nothing that is 'necessary' – dare I say more? I would rather commit a sin than compromise myself.

There are many different preliminary exercises to the Death Posture: they are all futile in themselves, but all lead to the Death Posture itself. The Death Posture is the reduction of all conception ('sin') to the 'Neither-Neither' state in which there is no more desire – only contentment by pleasing yourself. This is the only way of overcoming the inertia of belief, the only way of restoring the new sexuality, and the only way of attaining the ever-original self-love in freedom. The primordial vacuity is not attained by focusing the mind on a negation of conceivable things, such as the identity of unity and duality, chaos and uniformity, etc. It is attained by doing it now, not 'eventually'.[36] Perceive and feel without the necessity of what is opposite to a concept – think rather of what is related to it. Perceive light (metaphorically), not through its contrast with shadow, but by its own colour, through evoking the emotion of laughter at the time of ecstasy in union, and by practising until that emotion is subtle and continuous. The law of reaction is defeated by inclusion. If you were to enjoy a hundred pleasures at a time, however much your ecstasy, you will not lose, but a great increase takes place. Practice the Death Posture daily, until you arrive at the centre of all your desires: you will have imitated the great purpose. In this way, all emotions should find equilibrium at the time of emanation, until they become one.[37] Therefore, by hindering belief (and semen) from conception, emotions become simple and 'cosmic'.[38]

By the illumination of the Death Posture, there is nothing that cannot be explained: certainly I find satisfaction in ecstasy. I have now told you a very important secret, one that was known to me in childhood. Just by diligently striving for vacuity of belief, one becomes 'cosmic' enough to dwell in the innermost of other people and enjoy being 'them'.[39] Few men know what they really believe or desire: if you want to know, begin by locating your belief until you see the will that lies behind it.

Although belief and will form a duality, they are identical in their desire. There can be no control through will and belief, for they are forever at variance, and each tries to shape the other to its ends. However, neither wins in the end because it is only a cover for sorrow. You must therefore find a way of uniting them.

CHAPTER 6

The Cloudy Enemies Born of Stagnant Self-Hypnotism

"Natural Belief" is a form of belief compelled by intuition. Belief is thus compelled by what is experienced alternately reacting to, and dominating, the individual. Anything to be experienced has to associate with the individual through its own particular and appropriate form of emotion, stimulated by other factors in harmony with it. Emotions that are discordant lose harmony and inhibit. So by its own workings, Belief is limited and determined for you. The majority of our actions can be traced back to a subconscious desire for freedom that is in conflict with habit. This conflict is in obedience to an inherent fatalism which hangs on 'good and bad' actions already committed (in past experience) against an over-preserved and outmoded morality- the 'elemental' morality, or fear of displeasing [also known as the 'conscience']. This reaction is expressed as spontaneity, involuntariness, autonomy, the deliberate, etc., as the chance arises. The rest is due to a conflicting traditional moral doctrine that has become part of one's constitution (partly adopted to govern and time this reaction). It originates in an idea of what was previously considered conveniently good and bad. Thus, it is possible to maximise pleasure by an arbitrary compromise between abstinence from, and performance of, the desire feared.[40]

People absorb this traditional moral doctrine through the pretence of its divine origin. Its tenets are: reward for obedience, and punishment for transgression – both holding good for all time – in this world and the next. This moral code is a dramatic parody of the conceptive faculty, but is never so perfect or simple that it allows latitude for change in any sense. Thus it becomes dissociated from evolution [of the individual or society], and cannot change or adapt with circumstances. Because of this gradual divorce from purpose, it tends to lose its utility and is in danger of disappearing, but, in order to preserve itself, it does evolve contradictions or complications.[41] If we transgress its commandments, our 'dishonesty' suggests to us arguments for its iniquity for our self-justification. Alternatively, we might simultaneously create an excuse or 'reason' for the sin by a distortion of the moral code that allows some incongruity. (However, we usually do this while retaining a few 'unforgivable' sins – and an unwritten law). This negative confession is merely a fake rationalisation that allows casual excuses, a process of self-deception to satisfy and quickly re-persuade yourself of your own righteousness.

Which among any of us has any excuse but self-love? We fail to create or confess a morality that is convenient, lends itself to growth, remains simple, and allows transgression without excuse or punishment... it would not only be wise but common sense to do so. Everything eventually turns into its opposite, and through permanent association with the same moral code, we help desire to transgress. In desiring the things denied, the more you restrict, the more you sin. However, desire equally desires the preservation of moral instinct, so desire is its own conflict. Have no fear: the Bull of Earth[42] has long had nothing to do with your unclean conscience, your stagnant ideas of morality. The microbe alone would seem to be without fear.[43]

The Complexity of the Belief
(Know Thyself)

The idea of time is itself created by time. Through this artificial idea, the nature of belief becomes equal to all possibilities, so that which is not timely is not true, and which is not true is prediction. Any thought or idea automatically implies the possibility of its opposite. Belief is a way of trying to make one idea or the other the more convincing. The trouble with belief is the denial or limit it imposes upon the capabilities of the vitality or life-force. To believe at all is a form of 'brainwashing' to exclude the implied opposite by adopting a hypothesis or faith that can reflect on the rejected idea in a non-worrying way, or rationalises it deceitfully.

Truth is not the 'truth' of formula. The centre of belief is love for the Self, projecting one's environment as a means to fulfilment, but allowing distortions in it that simulate denial. One may have an ambition to become beyond self-desire, but one cannot get further than the centre, so one multiplies (believes) in order to become less aware of the fundamental. Now, this refusal to believe what one believes and exactly as one believes is the first condition for anyone who desires in any sense whatsoever: the man who is in love must of necessity become a liar, self-hypnotised by his morbid infatuation.[44]

You know the results... you can only 'truly believe' one thing, yet its continued involvement is essential (as the truth seems to kill, and does kill when feared), so the imagined seems to go on forever. The imagination learns that the idea is what compels it. To explain the 'why' of belief (or anything else), we must transcend its separation.

The way to do this is by a complete understanding of how the self loves. As we try to imitate the law of duality in our processes of believing, we realise that it may not be so simple as it seems. Who has transgressed the law of conception? Who has no fear? Yet, from the sin of conception, there comes a way of knowing what determines the nature of reality. Quietly expecting disappointment at the time of desire becomes the means of finding out where its deceit lies. Beyond it is something entirely arbitrary, the cause of delay, the ordainer of law, imitating the desire, but not caring about the consequences. 'Reason' is belief, which is fear of one's own capabilities, the faith that one is not even all the wonders of creation, let alone the Creator itself. It is delay[45]... belief well earns the terrible hatred of the vitality or life-force: belief is never freedom!

Belief creates its own necessary experience, and progress originates in retrogression: consider that 'reality' is somewhere, and the scope of your belief may be too small for it to inhabit! Oh, ye of much faith in God, replace it gradually by the worship of Self!

Ah, foolish man, learn to worship the glorious in freedom. When death approaches, faith in God and your desire of women will not save you... what use are they when withering and decay sets in and the body becomes an object of disgust? And what is the use of knowledge and charity when the nature of reality is known? Unsheathe the sword of the Self: ideas of the Almighty should be constantly slain, and the nature of 'righteousness' should be questioned. If you study the nature of your true self a little, the 'self' will begin to study you. You can compel anything to happen without causing offence: just as lustful tendencies tend to cease before the prospect of publicity and death, so do morals and faith tend to dissolve before the prospect of perfect bliss; when the desire is without fear or possessiveness, and the thought is fulfilled by vision, then a glimpse of the truth is born from purity of love. The fire that is all pleasure is released at will, and one becomes attraction itself, the pole-star towards which women steer.

When the believing principle is devoid of faith and ideas of God, then one becomes indestructible. Only when there is no fear in any form can there be any realisation of one's identity with reality itself (i.e. freedom). Then there will be no danger in negligence, since there is then no discrimination: for the person who is conscious of the slightest differentiation there will be fear. So long as there is any perception of self-reproach or conscience, there is some kind of pain germinating, and there is no freedom. He who believes anything he perceives or imagines, falls into sin. But by believing without worrying, and by forgetting ideas of what is internal and what external, he comes to regard everything as Self, is conscious of no resistance and no horizon, and is free.

On seeing the star-lit eyes and rosebud mouths, the breasts and loins of beautiful women, you become lovingly attached, but if you fear, consider that they are merely the charred flesh and bones of yourself after the torture. The space between the 'eternal' and the 'self': is it not merely a moral doctrine?

If you set about unbelieving all that you believe diligently and without anxiety (by the 'Neither-Neither' process), the principle of belief becomes simple and cosmic enough to include what you are always desiring, and you are free to believe what was impossible.

The desire is so mighty, it does not bother to ask permission, and suffers no consequences apart from the ecstasy of its possession. Against it, nothing can prevail. It burns up, like celluloid cast into a furnace, the old folly of promising things on behalf of an imagined 'another'. At hand is the freedom of Heaven: the Way, the Truth and the Light, and none dare say this of himself, but only by me. In truth alone I am 'Self', and my will, conditioned, is magical. Those who have lived much in their nature will in some degree be familiar with such a sensation, poor though it may be.

CHAPTER 7

Preface to Self-Love

L et us be honest! You are 'that', supreme in
freedom, most desirable, beyond desire,
untouched by the six stupefiers.[46] The sexuality
labours so that death may harvest by desire.
The elusive fancies of the senses are dangerous,
because of the 'righteousness' by which you have
learned to obey and control them. Hell-fire burns
because you conceived, and will only cease to hurt
when you succeed in identifying the Ego with all
possibilities by 'believing' through the 'Neither-
Neither' process. You are fire yet you are scorched!

Because you have willed belief, the cycle of
belief goes on and always obliges – so one day you
will have to believe differently, and the fire will no
longer hurt. Are you perhaps then saved, or are

there other ways of hurting you? We are talking about a state that 'is not'. In it, there is no sense that you are 'That' (Kiā) which is superb, and beyond the range of definition... there is no temptation of freedom, because 'It' was not the cause of evolution. Hence 'It' is beyond time, consciousness or unconsciousness, everything or nothingness, etc. This I know through the 'Neither-Neither', which is automatically beyond every conception, forever free in every sense. Perhaps 'it' may become less obscure by continual afterthought and vaguely felt through the hand of innocence – but whoever understands such simple meanings? It is never actually perceived: the ecstasy of the 'Neither-Neither' is imperceptible: it is always present, but the process of exhaustion hides it through the cycle of unity.

The certainty of consciousness is always the uncertainty of the perceived or experienced. This constant doubt spells fear, pain, decay, and the like, and is the cause of evolution, the eternal incompletion. O Desire, listen! Spiritual desire is as fatally virulent as sensuous desire. Aspiration towards a 'supreme' is a network of deadly desires because of cowardice within. Therefore, there is always some unsatisfied wisdom awaiting exploitation to experience its evolutions. There is no final wisdom: there is no final desire. How can anything end? Has today ever ended? These things are endlessness! A person desires things of this world – but what is the difference between this and desiring the 'Supreme Bliss'? Which is the more selfish? Which is nearer you? Which pleases the Creator more? Are you certain of the Creator's will and are you sure of your own desire?

Are you the Creator or just yourself, as you fondly imagine your contents? All these desires, however mighty, you will one day experience in the flesh, or even photograph. These things exist – very soon you will have real spiritual photographs (unfaked), but not by the camera you use at present.[47] The pioneer is ever the old fool. An afterthought – some spirits are already photographed: the microbes.[48]

Are you ever free from desire? Belief is eternal desire! Desire is its own cruelty, the restraint of the hand to labour in some unknown world: nothing is always dead, and no thought dies: the master becomes the slave, and vice versa. You have long believed this: it is in the flesh of your generations, together with the most merciless judge! You are faced with either the scorn of all your reforms or the inversion of your values! This constant curse and blasphemy: isn't the relief more in the knowledge of the newly-born and unrelenting taskmaster?

Are not our bodies all smeared with the blood of desire? Has not the world always been bloody from it? Are not our pleasures just a rest in order to drink the blood of slaughter? Oh, you determined liars: you know not yet the 'lie': it may be Truth!

The Ego is desire, so everything is ultimately both desired and undesirable. Desire is ever a preliminary forecast of terrible future dissatisfaction that is hidden by its ever-present vainglory. The Millennium will come and quickly go. Men will be greater than all the gods they ever conceived, yet there will be greater dissatisfaction.[49] You are ever what you always were, but may be so in a different form! A person or a nation, however vain or content, falls immediately into unknown and inevitable desire, consuming themselves little by little as a result of external conditions.

The mind becomes firm in desire by treating desire as devotion, but when the desire is realised, does it then become eternally desirable – or even desirable for just a million years? In heaven, your foot will be restrained![50] Therefore remove the conception that desire is 'pure' or 'impure', or ever finds completion: remove it by means of the 'Neither-Neither'. Even if the desire is for exhaustion of desire by the 'Neither-Neither' or for realization in the form of a wife, it is still desire, and unending evolution. Therefore remove desire in any form by means of the 'Neither-Neither'. Remove the illusion that there is 'Spirit' and 'Not-Spirit' (an idea that has never given beneficial results),[51] and remove all other conceptions by the same means. So long as the notion remains that there is 'compulsory bondage' in this world or even in dreams, then there is such bondage. Remove the conception of freedom and bondage in any world or state by meditation or 'Freedom in Freedom' by the 'Neither-Neither'.

For this we know: Vampirism is quite well proven enough. It is at least true in the case of vampire bats, quite apart from the possibility of it occurring through a divine or human agency. Therefore one should Kiā-ize desire by the 'Neither-Neither'. This is the most excellent formula that lies far beyond mere contentment, the all-embracing vacuum that reduces 'all' to common sense and upon which this universe rests. Therefore, believe nothing in this book through the 'Neither-Neither', dispel the conception of the 'Neither-Neither' by the 'Neither-Neither', and believe it is 'not necessary', and conclude by pleasing yourself, because 'does-not-matter-need-not-be'.

One believes this all the time as the truth of 'The Will', not of the thing believed, since the means to an end mean evolution to endless means.

In that remarkable state of simplicity, there is no beginning or end to wisdom or of anything – so how can it be related to conception and intelligence?

CHAPTER 8

Self-Love as a Moral Doctrine and Virtue

The standards for judging an action are: freedom of movement, timeliness of expression, and the pleasure it gives. The value of a moral doctrine is the freedom it allows for transgression. Simplicity I hold most precious. Are not the simplest things in the world also the most perfect, pure, and innocent? Aren't their properties the most wonderful?[52] Hence, simplicity is the source of wisdom. Wisdom and happiness are the same.

In love, pleasing my Self needs no excuse: is this not perfection? If actions exhibited their conformity to the Great Purpose, they would appear unfathomable and incomprehensible. There are few who can attain this, for who has no shame? Ecstasy in satisfaction is the Great

Purpose. Freedom from the necessity of law, realisation simply by wishing, is the ultimate law. Law depends on two: two is abundance, but as for millions... well, law is complicated. The second did not agitate, the first did not determine, nor was it compelled or preferred.

'Chance' in sport is not regarded as prophecy, but by its study, we have gained enough proficiency to determine an outcome with a certain degree of confidence. Prepare for the Eternal, revert to simplicity, and you are free.

What man can give without a degree of impulse – only the man whose sexuality is complete? The highest goodness is self-nourishment. What are we going to include as 'self'? Perfect charity acquires, hence it benefits all things by not giving.

What man can have faith without fear – only the man who has no duty to perform? When faith perishes, then so does duty to moral doctrines, for us who are without sin and endure forever in all-enduring love.[53]

What man can know with certainty – only he who has rubbed out the necessity of learning? When teachers fall out with each other, what is the use of learning from them? The wise are non-contentious and have no dogma to expound; rather they are as silent as a new-born babe when feeding.

What teacher can show the source of his wisdom? It is because I know without learning; I know the source and can convey lessons without teaching. Knowledge is but the excrescence of experience: experience is but its own repetition. The true teacher implants no knowledge, but shows the pupil his own superabundance. Keeping his vision clear, he directs or leads his pupil to the essential. Having shown him the source of wisdom, he retires before gratitude or sentiment towards himself set in, leaving the pupil to use wisdom as he wishes. Is not this the way of Heaven? He who trusts in his natural fund of genius has no knowledge of its boundaries, but as soon as he doubts, ignorance obsesses him. Doubt germinates in the virgin soil, and he becomes a coward to difficulties.

The difference between genius and ignorance is the degree of fear. The beginning of wisdom is a fear of knowledge-learning. Children doubt and abhor learning. Even pretending to be courageous results in cleverness![54]

The difference between good and evil is a matter of profundity. Which is nearer you, self-love and its immorality, or love and morals? Self-love is not conscious of 'deserving', so it is the equal of heaven, and enjoys constant happiness in wisdom.

From self-glorification and self-exaltation we arise superior from the incapacity that results from fear. From this position, we can ridicule to the point of destruction the notion of humility in repentance.

This self-love that does not give but is glad to receive is a genuine opportunity for freedom from covetousness, from the militant amusement of heaven. He who sublimates animal instincts to reason quickly loses control. Are not the animals we see in circuses trained by torture? And do not the animals reared in love eventually slay their master? The wise embraces and nourishes all things, but does not act as a master. Only when passions are ruled by foreign environment do they become dangerous. Control is by leaving things to work out their own salvation. Directly we interfere with other things and beings, we become identified with and subject to their desire.[55] There is peace when the Ego becomes the seer in the state of self-love.

Directly we desire, we have lost all. We are what we desire, and therefore we never obtain. Desire nothing and there is nothing you will not realise. Desire is desire for completion: the inherent emotion that is 'all happiness', all wisdom, and in constant harmony. But directly we believe, we become liars, and identified with pain. But pain and pleasure are one and the same. Therefore believe nothing, and you will have reverted to a simplicity that childhood has not yet attained. The fool asks 'how' – as we must believe in pleasure and pain. Now, if we could experience pleasure and pain at the same time, whilst holding fast to a principle that ascends, and allows the Ego to vibrate at a level above them, will we not have reached a state of ecstasy? Now, belief is the 'Ego', yet separates the Ego from Heaven, in the same way as your body separates you from another's.

Therefore by retaining a belief in the 'not necessary' (when conceiving), the Ego is free. The emotion of laughter is exhaustion: it is the primordial experience. So by invoking the emotion of laughter at the point of unity (of sex, or of anything), it is possible to unite pain and pleasure and experience them both simultaneously. By the 'not necessity' of one's belief, one's conception transcends this world and reaches the absolute ecstasy.

There is then no place where pain or death can enter. The idea of God is the primordial sin, and all religions are evil. Self-love, however, is its own law, which may be broken with impunity because it is not servile to anything else, but serves its own ever-ready purpose. Surely it is all that is left to us that involves no sin and is free? Verily, it is the only thing that we dare to be conscious of. He that truly pleases himself is without virtue, and shall satisfy all men. Hate, jealousy, murder, etc., are conditions of love, even as virtue, greed, selfishness, etc., are conditions of not pleasing oneself. There is no sin more sickening than love, for it is the very essence of covetousness, and the mother of all sin – hence it has the most devotees. Only self-love is pure: it does not have many followers. He that entirely loves himself induces self-love only. In this he is unstoppable, but does not offend like other men. He is like the great purpose, his actions explained for him, good seen of his evil, and without knowing, everyone satisfied with his will. Do not Heaven and Earth unite daily in spontaneous homage to this will of self-love? No man can show greater self-love, than by giving up all he believes.

Why do I value this self-love before all else? Is it not because I may be free to believe in evil but have no thought that anyone can do me injury? All is self-love, and the people of the world, if only they knew, are its devotees. My new law is the great clue to life. If the world could understand this, the rotten fabric would be discarded, and they would diligently follow the way in their own hearts, so there would be no further desire for 'unity': try and imagine what that implies. May the idea of 'God' perish and with it 'Woman': they have both made me look clownish.[56] Let there be no mistake, purity and innocence are simplicity, and happiness is wisdom. What is simple has no duality.

CHAPTER 9

The Doctrine of Eternal Self-Love

S elf-love is the completion of belief. The 'self' is the 'Neither-Neither', nothing omitted, indissoluble, beyond prepossession; dissociation of conception by its own invincible love. In it, Desire, Will and Belief cease to exist as separate. When attraction, repulsion and self-control are continued, they become the original unity, inert in pleasure. In this state, there is no duality, and no desire for unity: the dual principle rests in its unmodified state. The belief is no longer subject to conception because it conceives 'self' as such by loving. At other times, the 'Neither-Neither' creates a centre, becomes its environment, and becomes identified with its ramifications. At these times, conception has created, and becomes subject to law and the insatiable desire for unity, inasmuch as the duality is unity. At this point it should be pointed out that the 'Neither-Neither' emanates a Tetragrammaton of relativities, the sexes of which are evolved through their reflections in the form of a cross, and which are difficult to identify. In their fusion they produce unity (duality) and acquire conception. Multiplying by subdivision they embrace eternity, and in their manifold ramifications is law.[57]

Servitude to law is the hatred of Heaven.[58] Only self-love is the eternal all-pleasing, which is achieved by meditation on this radiant self which is mystic joyousness.

At that time of bliss, he is in time with his imagination: in that day, what happiness is his! He is a lusty innocent, beyond sin and without hurt! Balanced by an emotion, a rainbow-like refraction of his ecstasy is all he is aware of as external to himself. His vacuity causes a double refraction, and 'he', the self-radiant, illuminates the ego. He is beyond law, and is the guest at the 'Feast of The Supersensualists'.[59]

He has power over life and death, and this is the test: the one who doubts would naturally submit himself to himself. Though saved by this, he is still not beyond self-reproach, for truly he has unleashed all the trouble of the world, and the murder from the lightning. Self-love, in preventing the mind from concentration, is identity without form and is not thought as such: law and external influences are contained, and do not affect it. When that giving-up of all belief reflects only its own meaning, then there is purity of vision and innocence of touch, i.e. self-love. Truly, men are born, suffer and die through their belief. Ejaculation is death. Self-love is preservation and life.

Man, in order to invoke pleasure in his choice, actually subtracts from desire: his desire is partial desire, and becomes sub-double (resulting in conflict) and his energy is never full. Having no true focus, he is deceived in his strength, and attains a pure measure of pleasure from his body. He may be successful, but how heavy is his sentence! Pleasure becomes the illusion. Through dire necessity, 'his means', he is bound to its cause and effect, and is burnt as a sacrifice on the pyre of sentiment. This self-love is the only full energy, all else just a wrapping of dissatisfaction, an assumption of desires which only obscures. Man in the misery of his illusions and unsatisfied desires flies to different religions and deceptions, to re-deceive and re-hypnotise himself, a cover-up operation as a result of which he suffers fresh miseries when these new beliefs themselves become exhausted.

The terms of this attempted cure are new illusions, greater entanglement, and a yet more stagnant environment. Having studied all means to pleasure and pondered upon them again and again, I have found this self-love to be the only free, true and full form of love: nothing is more sane, pure and complete. There is no deceit: when by this means all experience becomes known for certain, and everything becomes sublimely beautiful and exceedingly good-natured, where is the necessity of other means? Like drink to the drunkard, everything should be sacrificed for it. This self-love is now declared by me to be the means of evolving millions of ideas for pleasure without love, or its synonyms: self-reproach, sickness, old age, and death. The Symposium of Self and Love. O! Wise Man, Please Thyself.

CHAPTER 10

The Complete Ritual and Doctrine of Magic

Ecstasy in Self-Love the Obsession

My dearest, I will now explain the only safe and true formula, the destroyer of the darkness of the world, the most secret among all secrets. Let it be secret to him who would attain. Let it cover any period of time, depending on what he conceives. There is no qualification required: the means are simplicity itself, so the practitioner is comparatively free to make his own qualifications and difficulties – i.e. 'magical retirements' are absurd and will only prove his incapacity, the non-existence of which he sets about to prove. He at once sets his limit and his servility. The practitioner's very existence symbolises all that is necessary for perfection.

Most emphatically, there is no need for repetition or feeble imitation. You are alive! True magic involves the reduction of properties to simplicity – making them transmutable so that they can be utilized in fresh directions, bearing fruit many times. Know deliberation, self-consciousness and concentration to be antithetical to magic, and sycophancy to be a way of making stupid. Whether for his own pleasure and power, the fulfilment of desire is the magician's purpose – magic is thus a means of ending his desire. Let him wait for some natural desire analogous in intensity, then sacrifice this desire (or its fulfilment) to the initial desire. By this means, the initial desire becomes 'organic'[60] and of the desired amount. The typical practitioner has probably not yet attained freedom from the law of duality, but not to worry: this is a short formula that will work for those whose belief is still full in the law, and are householders following their desires. The formula holds good for any purpose.

So let the practitioner wait for a belief to be subtracted, when some disillusionment has taken place – e.g. the loss of faith in a friend, or a union that does not fulfil expectations. So verily, disappointment can become his opportunity! This 'free entity of belief' and his desire are united to his purpose by the use of Sigils, or sacred letters. By projecting consciousness into one object, sensation becomes intensified because not dissipated by the usual distractions. This intensification is attained by abstaining from desire in anything but the object [i.e. the Sigil]. By non-resistance (involuntary thought and action), any worry or apprehension of it not working, being transient, find no permanent abode, and the practitioner desires everything. Anxiety defeats the purpose, because it retains and exposes the desire; desire is non-attraction. When the mind is quiet and focused, and undisturbed by external images, there is no distortion of the sense impression (there should be no hallucination: that could end in fulfilment of whatever it is that is imagined). Instead, the mind magnifies the existing desire, and joins it to the object in secret.

Casting the Shadow

Since the Ego is not totally oblivious, let the practitioner retain and visualise only the sigil form. It may be regarded as his chalice, the means of vacuity and incarnation. By considering an analogous emotion at that time, he substitutes for the law. He works a miracle, and imitates to the point of attainment a balance unknown in this world. As all other consciousness is annulled with safety, and the vehicle is strong enough for the ecstasy, he is beyond hurt. Now let the practitioner imagine within himself the mystic union of the Ego and Absolute. When the resulting nectar of ecstasy is emitted, let him drink of it again and again. If this sexual ecstasy manifests itself physically, let him imagine another's body; he has that Sigil for just such an emergency. Although this is not the primary purpose of the exercise, he will find it exceedingly agreeable. After this astonishing experience his passion is incomparable: there is nothing in the world he will desire unless he wills. That is why people do not understand me. The ecstasy in its emotion generates everything. Know it as the nectar of life, the Syllabub[61] of Sun and Moon. Verily he steals the fire from heaven: the greatest act of bravery in the world.

However, there is a risk here: if the desire remains part of the conscious Ego, there will be a dangerous moment of vulnerability, and the new desire [which should have been forgotten, and completely contained within the Sigil], may become a presiding obsession. This is because control has been surrendered to the energy of the original disappointed desire, which finds itself momentarily free from its original law, thus generating double personality (insanity).

By these means, however, there is no desire that is beyond fulfilment and no accomplishment too wonderful: it all depends on the amount of free belief. It may be achieved by localizing desire to just one sense. So for example, if you used the ear as the vehicle, one would hear the most transcendent music ever conceived, being the voices and harmony of every conceivable animal and human existence... it is the same with each sense. Oh, you men of small pleasure and enterprise, oblivious to your purpose, fault-finding, avaricious and sinful, who cannot live without women and cannot enjoy without pain, fearsome, inconstant, diseased and withered, dependent, cruel, deceived and liars, the worst of men! Know, O Lord, O beloved Self, I have now told you of that most secret tavern where passion goes when youth has gone, where any man may drink of the nectar of all-beneficial and gratuitous ecstasy. It is the most pleasurable nourishment that harms no-one.

CHAPTER 11

Note on the Difference Between Magical Obsession (Genius) and Insanity

Magical obsession is that state of mind when the mind is illuminated by sub-conscious activity evoked voluntarily by means of deliberate magical formula at a time of our own choosing, for the purpose of inspiration. It is the condition of genius. Any other form of obsession is a matter of 'the blind leading the blind', known as mediumism, a passive opening out of the ego to any external influence, elementals or disembodied energy. Such a transmuted consciousness actually constitutes a resistance to 'true' unconscious activity. It is a form of voluntary insanity, a sleep-walking of the Ego with no kind of form or control to guide it, hence its emanations tend to be either stupid in suggestion, or memories of childhood.

The form of obsession known as insanity is the memory of an experience that is dissociated from the personality (Ego) through some sort of rejection.[62] It is 'sub-crystalline', i.e. amorphous, and cannot become permanently attached to the sub-consciousness, as long as it has not exhausted or completed itself by realisation. Depending on its degree of intensity and the resistance shown to it at some time or other, the Ego may or may not have knowledge of the obsession. Its expression is always autonomous, and divorced from personal control, power of direction and timing. Concentration determines dissociation from the Ego.

Enthusiasm for one object[63] seeks completion by identification with it, and either sacrifices all else to it, or deliberately forgets it. It is separated from the Ego by its own intensity or the shock of resistance determined by some incompatibility with the desire. If it ever becomes equal, or greater than the rest of the consciousness, it causes subdivision or 'double personality'.

Concentration on some fixed idea is dissatisfied desire, a conflict that can never be satisfied, because of the ineffectual means used in the attempt to overcome it. It occurs when the Ego either appears not to have or does not know the means of fulfilment or transmutation to escape the desire that worries it. None of these leads to the annihilation of the desire or obsession, but only its separation or concealment from the rest of the Ego, giving it a premature sub-conscious existence. It is held there only when some form of resistance is active, for when resistance becomes dormant, control is given to the presiding obsession, allowing its incarnation in, and swamping of the Ego, which has to live and perform its emotional experience. Disease and insanity (all disease is insanity)[64] is caused when the disembodied energy has no vital function. However, this energy can be put to good use in the vitalisation of sigils.

CHAPTER 12

Sigils

The Psychology of Believing

If the 'supreme belief' remains unknown, believing is fruitless. If 'The Truth' has not yet been ascertained, the study of knowledge is unproductive. Even if 'they' were known, their study is useless. We are not the object by perceiving it, but by becoming it. Closing the gateways of sense is of no help. Verily I will make common-sense the foundation of my teaching. Otherwise, how can I convey my meaning to the deaf, vision to the blind, and my emotion to the dead? In a labyrinth of metaphor and words, intuition is lost: therefore without using them, you must learn the truth about oneself from him alone who knows the truth... yourself. Of what use is the

wisdom of virginity to him who has been raped by
the seducer, ignorance? Of what use are sciences
or any knowledge except as medicine? Hidden
treasure does not come at your word or by digging
with your hands in the main road. Even with the
proper implements and accurate knowledge of
place, etc., you may just end up re-acquiring what
you possessed long ago. There is a great doubt as to
whether it is hidden, except by the strata[65] of your
experiences and atmospheres of your belief.

So how does one become a genius? My reply is like
the mighty germ: it is in agreement with the Universe,
is simple and full of deep import, yet it is for a time
extremely objectionable in terms of your ideas of
good and beauty. So listen attentively, O aspirant, to
my answer, for by living its meaning you shall surely
become freed from the bondage of constitutional
ignorance. You must live it yourself: I cannot live it
for you. The chief cause of genius is the realization of
'I' by an emotion that allows the instant assimilation
of what is perceived. This emotion could be called
'immoral' in that it allows the free association of
knowledge without being encumbered by belief. Its
condition is therefore ignorance of 'I am' and 'I am
not': instead of believing, there is a kind of absent-
mindedness. Its most excellent state is the 'Neither-
Neither', the free or atmospheric 'I'.

Do you remember thinking in your youth [perhaps especially whilst on journeys] that 'this world is a curious place', following the feeling you got upon asking yourself whether this life is a reasonable development? What was the cause of this – and what was the cause of you dismissing it summarily from your mind? Related to it is the feeling that the most commonplace object is magnificently strange, and the vague feeling that there is a co-relation between the incompatible (exhaustive arguments often see this, but always excuse it) and the curiosity and shock that come from a more intimate association with the wonders of creation. What is it that prevents you from following with an investigation into 'what exactly is surprise', etc.? What is the cause of you believing more in God than in a dog-fight? Yet you fear dogs more than God! Where is the difference between you in the condition of being choked with disquieting piety, and the innocence of a babe? Perhaps in these we can look for the cause of ignorance.

Belief is the fall from the Absolute. What are you going to believe? Truth seeks its own negation. Different aspects are not the truth, nor are they necessary to truth. Which of its emanations are you to strangle at birth? In this sense, are you

illegitimate? You believe in right and wrong-
so what punishment will you determine? Can
you escape the driving 'must'? Who can escape
boredom- without change? Who can remain single
and content? What man among you is large and
free enough to encompass his 'self'? Your belief
obscures lineage. 'Ambition' is really smallness,
as it is related to the accustomed environment in
which you find yourself. Remember, time is an
easy, natural and spontaneous imagination of the
experienced. What may be called the primordial
experience was its completion, so there is no end to
learning. What you learn tomorrow is determined
by what you have done, so is the accomplished
lesson of yesterday. Never learning today what you
can do tomorrow is called loss, but is theft from
time, wholesomeness and rejuvenation. Repeat
this delay again and again until you arrive at
spontaneity, and can accept chance in safety. The
pursuit of learning by believing is the grotesque
incubator of stupidity.

If you could truly believe, it would be possible
to see some virtue in it. We are not free to
believe, however much we desire to, because we
have conflicting ideas that we have to exhaust
first. Sigils are the art of believing; my invention
for making belief unconscious[66] and therefore

true belief. A wish to believe something is of necessity incompatible with the existing belief it is to replace, and cannot be realized through the inhibition of the unconscious belief – the negation of the wish. Faith moves no mountains, not until it has removed itself. Supposing I wish to be 'great' (nevermind that I am): to have 'faith' and believe that I am does not make me great, even if I were to keep up the pretence to the end... it would be ceremonial insincerity, the affirmation of my incapacity. I am incapable, because that is the true belief, and the one imprinted on my unconscious. To believe differently is but affectation. Therefore imagining or having 'faith' that I am 'great' is a superficial belief. The reaction and denial is caused by the troublesome welling up of the unconscious incapacity. Denial or faith does not change or annihilate it, but reinforces it and preserves it.

Therefore belief, to be true, must be unconscious. The desire to be 'great' can only become unconscious at a time of vacuity[67] and by giving it (Sigil) form. If you become conscious of the Sigil form at any time (other than in a specifically magical context), you should suppress it, by deliberately striving to forget it. By this means it becomes active and dominates the unconscious: its form is nourished and is allowed to become attached to the unconscious mind. It thus becomes an unconscious belief, and once this has been accomplished, it has a chance to be realized and become reality. You become your concept of 'greatness'.[68]

So belief becomes true and vital by striving against it in consciousness and by giving it form. Not by the striving of faith. Belief exhausts itself by confession and non-resistance, i.e., consciousness. Believe not to believe, and in degree you will obtain its existence. At a time depending on your morality, give to the poor. If the ambitious only knew it is as difficult to become incapable as it is to become great. They are mutual as accomplishments and equally satisfying.

CHAPTER 13

The Sub-Consciousness[69]

All geniuses have an active unconscious, and the less they are aware of the fact, the greater their accomplishments. The unconscious is exploited by desire reaching it. So consciousness should not contain the desire for 'greatness' once the Ego has wished: and should be filled with an affected ambition for something different, not vice-versa.[70] Since the inevitable penalty of cowardice lurks somewhere, surely this is not an inglorious deceit? Genius, like heroism, is a matter of bravery – you have to forget fear or incapacity somehow... hence the expression of genius is always spontaneous. How simple it is to acquire genius: you know the means, yet who will take the plunge? The learning of 'How' is the eternal

'Why' – unanswered! A genius is such, because he does not know how or why.

The Storehouse of Memories with an Ever-Open Door

Know the unconsciousness to contain all experience and wisdom, past incarnations as men, animals, birds, vegetable life, etc. – everything that exists, has and ever will exist, each being a stratum in the order of evolution. Naturally then, the deeper we probe into these strata, the earlier will be the forms of life we arrive at; the last we find is the Almighty Simplicity. And if we succeed in awakening them, we may gain their properties, and our accomplishments will correspond to them. Since they are experiences long past, they must be evoked by extremely vague suggestions, which can only operate when the mind is in an unusually quiet or simple state. To have their wisdom, we do not need their bodies. The body is modified relatively to the 'means' available (we humans travel faster than the hunting leopard, but do not have its body), and when it is the means, it changes accordingly. Now, if we observe Nature, the earliest forms of life are wonderful with respect to their properties, adaptability, etc.; their relative strength is enormous, and some are indestructible. No matter what the desire of some species of organism is, it always becomes its accomplishment. A microbe has the power to destroy the world (and certainly would if it took an interest in us).

If you were to remove the limb of some primitive organism, the part would re-grow, and so forth. So by evoking and becoming obsessed by these former existences, we can gain their magical properties, or the knowledge of their attainment. This is what already happens, though, albeit very slowly (everything happens all the time): in striving for knowledge we repel it; the mind works best on simplicity.

The Key to Prophecy

The law of evolution consists of the regression of function governing the progression of attainment: in other words, the more wonderful our attainments, the lower the scale of life that governs them. Our knowledge of flight is determined by the desire to fly activating the Karmas within us of birds and other flying animals. Directly our desire reaches the unconscious stratum belonging to those existences that involved flight without wings, then we shall fly without machines. This unconscious activity is the 'capacity', the 'knowledge'; anything else we acquire is of negative or no value.

Now, learning and acquiring knowledge by ordinary means does have one virtue: it can cause worry and disappointment to the point of exhaustion. By this means, the desire might accidentally reach the real abode of knowledge, i.e. the unconscious. Inspiration is always at a 'void' moment and most great discoveries accidental, usually brought about by exhaustion of the conscious mind [allowing the unconscious mind to come up with the 'bright idea'].

My formula and sigils for unconscious activity are the means of inspiration, capacity or genius, and the means of accelerating evolution. They represent an economy of energy and a method of learning by enjoyment. A bat first grew wings of the proper kind by its desire being 'organic' enough to reach the unconscious. If a desire to fly had been conscious, it would have had to wait until it could do so by the same means as us, i.e. by machinery.

All genius has an 'alternative aim' in the form of a hobby, which serves to temporarily distract the conscious mind, and prevent its interference with spontaneous expression. The great Leonardo's mathematics and other interests served to deceive him as to his true ends in just this way. Our lives are full of symbolism reflecting the predominant Karmas that govern us. All ornament, useless dress, etc., are of this nature (people derive pleasure from their identification with these things), and offer a means of identifying the governing Karmas.

The symbolism of crowning a man King is that he, representing God (on Earth) has reached the lowest strata of his unconscious – represented as unicellular organisms – which predominate in governing his functions. (Of course, those crowned King are never such in practice: they symbolise the 'hope,' not the reality). Hence the floral motifs and precious stones featuring in the design of a crown symbolise a monarch's relation to first principles. He is King who has reached the dual principle in its simplicity, the primordial experience which is all experience: he has no need of crowns or kingdoms.[71]

By means of sigils and the acquirement of vacuity, any past incarnation, experience, etc., can be summoned to consciousness. It may even happen in sleep in the form of dreams, but this means is very difficult. (Chapters on day and night dreaming for pleasure have been omitted.)[72] Total vacuity is difficult and unsafe for those governed by morality or complexes, i.e. whose belief is not entirely self-love; hence the need for sigils. Know all ritual, ceremony, and conditions to be arbitrary (you have yourself to please): in the end, they are just a hindrance and a confusion; their origin was as an amusement, but they were later used for the purpose of deceiving others from knowing the truth and inducing ignorance and ,as always, the high priests involved were the most deceived themselves. He who deceives another deceives himself much more. Therefore know the charlatans by their love of rich robes, ceremony, ritual, magical retirements, absurd conditions, and other stupidities too numerous to relate. Their entire doctrine is a boastful display, a cowardice hungering for notoriety; their standard everything unnecessary, their certain failure assured. Hence it is that those with some natural ability lose it by their teaching. They can only dogmatise, implant and multiply that which is entirely superficial. Were I a teacher I should not act as master since – as he would be knowing more [about his own unconscious resources] – the pupil could lay no claim to discipleship. Assimilating slowly, the pupil would not be conscious of his learning, and would not commit the vital mistake; without fear, he would accomplish with ease. The only teaching possible is to show a man how to learn from his own wisdom, and to utilise his ignorance and mistakes: not by obscuring his vision and intention by ideas of 'right' and 'wrong'.[73]

CHAPTER 14

Sigils: Belief with Protection

Magical Obsession

I will now explain the creation and use of Sigils: there is no difficulty about it; how pure and right it all is. By this system, you know exactly what (you believe) your Sigil must relate to. If you were to use any form stupidly, you might just conjure up exactly what you did not want – the mother of insanity – or much more likely, nothing at all. Since this is the only system, any result obtained other than by it is accidental. Also, you do not have to dress up as a 'traditional' magician, wizard or priest, build expensive temples, obtain virgin parchment, black goat's blood, etc., etc., in fact no theatricals or humbug are required.

Out of love for my foolish devotees, I invented it. All desire, whether for Pleasure, Knowledge or Power, that cannot find 'Natural' expression, can by Sigils and their formula find fulfilment from the unconscious. Sigils are the means of guiding and uniting the partially free belief or energy (i.e. a disappointed desire, not yet an obsession), with 'organic' desire. The Sigil ensures the desires' carriage and retention until its purpose is served in the unconscious self, and its means of reincarnation served in the Ego.

All thought can be expressed in visual form, to which it bears a true relationship. Sigils are monograms of thought, for the government of energy (all hereditary crests, monograms, etc., are Sigils and represent the Karmas they govern), relating to Karma; a mathematical means of symbolising desire and giving it form that has the virtue of preventing any thought and association with that particular desire (at the magical time). The desire is thus protected from detection by the Ego, which cannot then restrain or attach the desire to its own transitory images, memories and worries, but allows it free passage to the unconscious.

Sigils are made by combining the letters of the alphabet after a process of simplification.

For example, the word 'Woman' in Sigil form is ⧓ or ⧑ or ⧒, etc. The word 'Tiger' ⧔ or ⧕, 'Hat' ⧖, 'Come' ⧗, 'Moon' ⧘, 'It' ⧙ or ⧚, etc.

The idea is to obtain a simple form that can be easily visualised at will, yet has not too much pictorial relation to the desire. The true method has a much greater virtue, which cannot be explained briefly, being the secret of thought form, as degrees of suggestion, and what is in a name.[74] We have now agreed as to how a Sigil is made, and what virtue it has. Verily, whatever a person believes by sigils is the truth, and is always fulfilled. This system of sigils is believed by taking it up as a hobby at a time of great disappointment or sorrow. By Sigils I have endowed fools with wisdom, made the wise fools, have given health to the sick and weak, disease to the strong, etc. Now, if, for some purpose, you wanted the strength of a tiger, you would make a sentence such as: 'This my wish to obtain the strength of a tiger'. Sigilized ,this would be:

"This my wish ⧛ to obtain ⧜ the strength of a tiger ⧝".
Combined as one Sigil: ⧞ or ⧟.

Now by virtue of this Sigil, you are able to send your desire into the unconscious (which contains all strength); that having happened, it is the desire's realization by the manifestation of the knowledge or power necessary.

Note: there are six methods of Sigils employed in this book, each corresponding to different strata. The one shown here is illustrative and the fundamental idea of them all, from which anyone can evolve his own system. Conditions, etc., of necessity subsequently evolve themselves. Also, a person has more power of creation and originality with a limited means of expression.[75]

First, all consciousness except of the Sigil has to be annulled; do not confuse this with concentration – you simply conceive the Sigil any moment you begin to think. Vacuity is obtained by exhausting the mind and body by some means or other. A personal or 'traditional' means serves equally well, depending on temperament: choose the means that is most personally pleasant to you. Good examples are: mantras and yogic posture, women and wine, tennis, playing patience, or by walking and concentration on the Sigil, etc. Note: this 'vacuity' is not the passivity of mediumism which opens the mind to what is called 'external influence' – disembodied energy usually having no better purpose than to rap tables. There are many means of attaining this state of vacuity. I mention the most simple: there is no need to crucify yourself. Drugs are useless for this purpose, and smoking and laziness are among the more difficult methods to make work.

None of these methods are necessary to him who has (even symbolically) for a moment by the 'Neither-Neither' meditation, conquered the Dual principle (Conception) – his Ego is free from gravity. If the Sigil is made an obsession by continually looking at it or thinking about it, its realization may happen at any moment, in the form of inspiration. This is done by returning the mind to the Sigil when one is extremely worried: the time of exhaustion thereby becomes the time of fulfilment. At the time of exhaustion or vacuity, visualise and retain only the Sigil form – eventually it will become vague, then vanish, and success is then assured. By the Ego conceiving only the Sigil and not being able to conceive anything from it, all energy is focused through it, and the desire for identification carries it to the corresponding sub-conscious stratum – its destination.

The Sigil being a vehicle, it serves the purpose of protecting the consciousness from a direct manifestation of the (consciously unacknowledged) obsession. Conflict is avoided with any incompatible ideas and neither gains separate personality. The obsession is either gradually assimilated and becomes organic, or returns to its original abode, its purpose of illumination served. Hence, by means of Sigils, the mind becomes either illuminated by knowledge or obsessed with power, depending on the intensity of desire. This illumination or obsession comes from the specific Karma (i.e. the record of a particular existence and knowledge gained by the unconscious stratum) related to the desire, but not from recent experience or memory. Knowledge is obtained by the sensation that results from the unity of the desire and Karma. Power is obtained by its 'actual' resurrection and vitalization.

This knowledge leaves its stratum together with the energy or desire returning to the Ego. It escapes the Ego's resistance by associating with similar images, memories, or experiences received in this life, that the mind contains, and crystallises itself by their symbolism. Hence most illumination is in symbolic form, and must subsequently be translated into terms the Ego can understand.

CHAPTER 15

Symbolism

K now symbols to be the means of epitomising knowledge for its unconscious retention, where it gains wisdom by seeking analogies among all other observations.

So, a symbol works and gains knowledge from 'the conscious', the Sigil from the 'Unconscious'. (Remember that the memory can be regarded as the unconscious part of the consciousness, and that the two form a continuum). The Ego is ignorant towards both sigils and symbols, but they both give the Ego a flow of knowledge from themselves. All knowledge of ideas, gained by means of sigils, should be re-clothed in pure symbolism to designate and stimulate its own wisdom. Symbolism is also a means of accelerating and exhausting by living a belief instead of repressing it by choice rather than of necessity, which serves its own time. All begging, self-punishment, sacrifice, etc., is but an attempt to escape the law of reaction or Karma, and by symbolising the reading of these laws, they hope to take that power from nature. In fact, fakirs and beggars symbolise those incarnations that are unpleasant (due to them as punishment) from choice rather than necessity, believing that by this method they will escape further evil; hence they sacrifice to, and worship as deities, their past actions. Symbolism is a vital and easy means of expressing self-conscious knowledge, vision or sensation that is difficult to express simply in a few words. Symbolism in its nature is either an arbitrary or a true representation reduced to pictorial simplicity, which is analogous when a representation of an abstract.

Illustration: 'Man' symbolised by the arbitrary method could be ⃗ or anything else. This method is purely fictitious and does not serve any purpose except the effort of remembering, but eventually, as a result of the process of simplification, it is bound to approach some true representation of what it symbolises, economy forcing it to utility. Hence ⃗ becomes ⃗ then ⃗. By the other method, i.e. the pure and true pictorial representation, 'Man' symbolised is ⚛, or more simply △, △, △ or purely phallic would be ⊔, ⌐ or ♭. So both methods eventually arrive at the same symbol as script; with one means [the former], it is a question of time before it is of any use. To symbolise an abstract, such as, 'Passions are best controlled by innocence (non-resistance),' we seek an accepted analogy; that is 'the passions' could be represented by a tiger, 'innocence' by a child. Hence we make a symbol of a child with a tiger. By this simple key, there is no traditional symbolism worth the name that cannot be read, or present knowledge expressed. Also, by means of symbolism, the imagination of others can be stimulated to evolve their own wisdom, once they start to work along simple lines.

The basis of all symbolism is the expression of unconscious knowledge that may or may not be exploited, depending on necessity. The Egyptians, for example, could be called an 'unconscious' race, artistic as opposed to our scientific. To them, the Darwinian was no new theory, and they were already in possession of the 'Vital' knowledge that humans had evolved from animals, from the lower forms of life. They symbolised this knowledge in one great symbol: the Sphinx (hence its importance in their iconography) which, pictorially, represents humankind evolving from animal existence. Their numerous Gods – all partly animal, bird, fish, etc. – prove the completeness of that knowledge, but there was no necessity for them to carry it further as we have, for they knew all that was fundamentally important to them. The cosmogony of their Gods is proof of their knowledge of the order of evolution, and its complex progress from one single organism. So also is their knowledge of the planetary theory, the atomic theory, etc. In fact, their simple basis embraces all the possibilities of our Science. They knew that they still possessed the rudimentary faculties of all existences, and were partly under their control. Thus their past Karmas became Gods, good and evil forces, etc., and had to be appeased: from this kind of process, all moral doctrine, etc., is determined [across all cultures]. So all 'Gods' have lived (being ourselves) on earth, and when dead, their experience or Karma governs our actions in some degree: to that extent, we are subject to the will of these Gods. This explains fatalism. This is the key to the mystery of the Sphinx.

Art supplies all the material which Science exploits. Formula is subsequent to inspiration.

CHAPTER 16

Automatic Drawing as Means to Art

Art as 'Need-not-Be': The Vital Religion

The virtue of Art is that it can contradict any law of Science, and to be Art, it need not be true to Science. It teaches that composition, balance or proportion can be obtained by any principle or exaggeration, so points at freedom in a deliberation that already exists. Were you to say that a certain principle is bad as Art (or as composition, colour etc.), it would simply be the chance for originality, and you could make a wonderful Art by utilizing only the prohibited or 'bad' principle. The one law of Art is its own spontaneity, its pleasure and freedom. How mystic, pure and simple is its wish;

it has no idea of potential divinity! Decoration is its creed and vital allegory is its belief. Being the 'Free Morality,' it has no sin – then most assuredly Art is all we dare express without excuse. So what is not Art is either Science or a moral photography. True Art being inspiration, it is the symbolic formula of the science it does not admit.

Art suggests, so is the best medium for conveying wisdom: its very suggestion thinks freedom. Art is that beauty which may be born of anything, but not by a formula of balance or proportion is born beauty itself. Ugliness is that which the formula does not allow: hence there is never beauty without this ugliness which becomes transmuted by its superabundance.

Art is the instinctive application (to observations or sensations) of the knowledge latent in the unconscious. Bad Art (fundamentally weak, as in composition, etc.), arises when a law, code or mannerism (always something learnt) does not allow (by forgetting the necessary negligence) spontaneity. Only Art is Eternal Wisdom; what is not Art soon perishes. Art is the unconscious love of all things. 'Learning' will cease and Reality will become known when it comes to pass that every human being is an Artist.

Automatic Drawing

Automatic Drawing is a vital means of expressing what is at the back of your mind (the Dream Self) and is a quick and easy means to begin being courageously original – eventually it evolves itself into the coveted spontaneous expression and its safe omniscience is assured. (The Dwellers on the Threshold of the unconscious, in their suffering, literally constitute the conscience or 'live morality'. Hence all automatic drawing, in its beginning, is either sentimental or morbid: the Dwellers must not be feared, despite their apparent plausibility: otherwise, you express nothing better than your own displeasure).[76]

Automatic drawing is obtained by the Sigil formula simplified (first make the desire to draw 'organic') and is a means of expressing unconscious activity pictorially: it is the easiest of psychic phenomena to attain. The hand has to be trained to work freely and of itself, contrary to its accustomed habit. Practice making these and other simple forms, swiftly and continuously:

 etc.

Continue with a variety of directions and shapes, until you accomplish them without conscious guidance. Then allow the hand to draw of itself, i.e. 'scribble' with the least deliberation possible. (This should be a continuous line that evolves whilst avoiding a return to its origin, accompanied by a continual afterthought suggesting new movement, i.e. a dancing line).

 (Not as a giddy, circular whirl: this is a manifestation of the childish rebellion towards learning).

Eventually your scribble will evolve form, style and meaning. When the mind is oblivious to what is occurring on the paper, great success is assured. A good way of getting yourself into the right kind of trance beforehand is to look at your thumb in the light of a moonbeam, until it is opalescent and suggests a fantastic reflection of yourself: this is a means to great perfection, and extraordinary results may be obtained.[77]

The drawings are symbolic in their meaning or wisdom. To determine what you want to draw, such as a particular Karma or your idea of a horse, make that Sigil and retain the mind on it. By these means all past incarnations can be expressed, and all creations seen without stirring foot. Automatic drawings are also the means of symbolically visualising sensation, and most of the drawings in this book are such, and include my first effort (made about 1900). They are also a means of foretelling final results by deducting from past actions – which constitutes fortune-telling (chapters on omens, fortune-telling, and prophecy omitted).[78]

Automatic drawing is a cure for insanity because it exposes the wounded sentiment, allowing the consciousness to recognise what is obsessing, and thus reason and control can begin afresh.

Note on Sacred Letters

Sacred letters preserve belief from the Ego, so that the belief returns again and again to the unconscious, until its fullness breaks the resistance. Its meaning misses conscious intelligence, but is understood by emotion. Each letter [of the alphabet you will notice used in some of the illustrated portions of the book] in its pictorial aspect relates to a Sex principle, and its modifications make a complete whole.

Twenty-two in number, they correspond to a first cause: each is analogous to an idea of desire, and together they constitute a symbolic cosmogony.[79] Thus the third letter is: ⚭.

It represents the dual principle or conceptive faculty. By knowledge of the first letter, one is familiar with the whole alphabet, and the thousands they imply. Together, they are the knowledge of desire. They embrace a positive system of grammar which allows easy, non-conflicting expression, and a reading of difficult and complex principles; ideas that at present would normally escape conception.

CHAPTER 17

On Myself

Although conceiving, you have given no sign of life. In claiming yourself, which is a work of creating value, do you find nothing worth holding onto, nothing satisfying: is the realisation of your inhibition all? Reality would apparently be gained by self-effacement. How empty and incomplete this idea of 'self' is! Its stimulation to simulate reality lies in self-denial. More and more becomes evident: for instance, that these ugly mists of illusion are parental, and the cause of Heaven's hatred! That is why I fear to believe in God, for that would mean subordination to something that is merely an attribute, and an idea of self is not freedom of love! Probably, almighty is he who is unconscious of the idea of God.

Now, may the fierceness of my unity be your silence. Let it no longer be for me a question or an effort to express my doubts. Yet mankind forever doubts, plays tricks on himself, and pays for every pleasure, until he becomes as a millionaire. He does have one fear, though: that the punishment shall fit the size of his gain! The rich in dross, to cheat his conscience, affects humility, and speaks of himself as 'poor,' his possessions as 'burdens,' or of 'small account'! Of what consolation is the 'truth' in the day of weary waiting and watching, the restless striving, the imprisonment, the rack, and the horrors of every conceivable torture? When he becomes accustomed to all this, loses his hold on reality, and is no longer deterred, will he then create God and miseries afresh?

Recognise this folly of the world, deny your faith, renounce this bloody-sceptred God and confess. The completion of folly is the beginning of childhood, but of 'knowledge' there is no end. It was the straying that found the path direct.[80] From my childhood, I have never denied my invincible purpose. Oh, silent watcher, thou sleepless eye of the Universe, watch over the beginning of all my ideas. The misery of the world would seem eternal whilst I, in the midst, like an infant not yet smiling, am in an impervious state of purity in self-love, but I dare not claim its service! I am in eternal want of realisation, but poor though I may be, my contentment is beyond your understanding.

Although I'm an opinionist, I hesitate to advocate an argument or compromise myself by believing my own doctrines as such; may they always be their own purifiers! I'm afraid of 'knowledge' and may my belief be in its emptiness, indeed, its ignorance! Away from my daring to believe religions, doctrines, or creeds, so I shall hold the jewel of Truth. I am so cautious that I simultaneously deny that which I affirm, and hold fast to the 'not-necessity'. I am superseded by paradox, and without antecedent, and spontaneously, I revert to the Absolute, from which I can watch, in a detached way, both my own intoxication and control – the reaction of Karma.

How easy is the Way, since it would seem as though nothing should be said but all unsaid! May my words be few and pregnant with meaning! Alas, the futility of the idea of God has not yet reached its limit[81] and all men being liars, appear to be striving for its climax in insanity. I, alone, like one prematurely aged reason tottering on its throne, remain sane, in positive chastity, confessing no conscience, no morals – a virgin in singleness of purpose.

Notes

1   From Spare's late *The Living Word of Zos:* 'What is
     Art? The function of Art is the ornamentation of
     things and of life for pleasure or interest'.

2   In his earlier *Earth Inferno,* (1904) Spare quoted
     the *Rubaiyat of Omar Khayyam:*
          'I sent my soul through the invisible,
          Some letter of that after life to spell:
          And by and by my soul return'd to me,
          And answer'd I myself am Heaven and Hell'.

3   Note: from the Sri Sankaracharya's Vivekachu-
     damani: "He who has slain the shark of desire
     with the sword of supreme or mature dispassion,
     crosses the ocean of samsara without obstacles."
     Spare may also be alluding to Da'ath, or the 'Abyss'
     of the Qabalah. From *The New Living Qabalah* by
     Will Parfitt (a modern work, 1988): 'The Abyss,
     in which Da'ath resides, is the gulf or chasm
     between the noumenal (that is, spirit) and the
     phenomenal (everything except spirit). The Abyss

exists between what is real and what is illusionary, between the ideal and the actual, the potential and the manifest. Above the Abyss all opposites are reconciled – there is no duality above the Abyss. Below it everything is duality. The Abyss can also be described as the gulf separating the individual soul from its source.

It is said that unresolved and irrational elements of the individual 'exist' within the Abyss, which cannot therefore truly be crossed without these elements being completely resolved. It is also said that to cross the Abyss the Adept must leave everything behind, give up all that he or she is.'

A shark, of course, is a voracious predator and scavenger, in its element in the Abyss of the ocean.

4   In other words, religion has set up all the rules, and these people are just working within them, and what is worse, they are at risk of psychosomatic physical illnesses as a result of these suppressed 'imaginary sins'. In this, Spare may have been influenced by the then-popular New Thought movement, as championed by Phileas Quimby and his many followers, including the founder of 'Christian Science', Mary Baker-Eddy, and Frances Hodgson-Burnett, author of *The Secret Garden* (which carries a New Thought message). From Quimby's *What is Disease?* (1861): 'The curing of disease must be governed by a law. Sin or death is the transgression of that law, and when there is no law there is no transgression'.

5   From *The Tao-te Ching*: 'What makes a great state is its being (like) a low-lying, down-flowing (stream); – it becomes the centre to which tend (all the small states) under heaven. (To illustrate from) the case of all females – the female always overcomes the

male by her stillness. Stillness may be considered (a sort of) abasement'. From *The Tao-te Ching* by Lao-Tzu, translated by James Legge.

6   Spare is struggling in the language of his time to distinguish between the content and the structure of religions: what appears to divide them is their (relatively unimportant) content; what they have in common is their manipulative structure, their means of deceiving and governing.

7   Spare was fascinated by paradox, and was to return to the theme in later writings. *The Living Word of Zos* contains a long section 'On Paradox', in which he concludes: 'Paradox is a disease of fallacious vocabulary'. He also, incidentally, betrays a sophisticated awareness of the philosophical and rhetorical possibilities of grammatical ambiguity!

8   This passage, probably the best-known in the book, is in clear enough English, so I have let it stand unchanged. For the benefit of newcomers, many of the remarks made in it appear to be thinly-veiled criticisms of Aleister Crowley, with whom Spare fell out during the course of writing the *Book of Pleasure*.

9   In other words, although our natures may be conveniently mapped onto the Qabalistic Tree of Life as an aid to understanding, the map should not be mistaken for the territory.

     Alternatively, Spare may be thinking of the phylogenetic trees drawn up by evolutionists such as Ernst Haeckel, to map humankind's evolutionary descent, and still much debated in Spare's time.

10   In other words, the unconscious mind will take the 'path of least resistance' in communicating with the conscious mind, so that in dreams, for example, it

will attempt to convey meaning through symbols with which the dreamer is most familiar – so to the modern dreamer, the archetypal theme of 'life's journey' is more likely to appear in the form of a railway journey than as a journey in a horse-drawn chariot. Hence Spare's injunction about 'observing your own functions': these will provide clues about what will be the most potent form of symbolism for you, and would be worth bearing in mind, e.g. when preparing Sigils.

11   This sceptical attitude towards conventional medicine is again, very 'New Thought'. See (5) above, and note the reference to a 'law'.

12   Spare's friend Frank Letchford provides a clue to interpreting this: in *Michelangelo in a Teacup* (1995) he says of Spare, 'His metaphysical theory was that our conditions are caused by our subconscious desires, and the subconscious, being all-wise, wills the environment that strengthens the weak places of the soul'. (p129)

13   Compare the *Tao-Te Ching* by Lao-Tsu:
'The Tao that can be trodden is not the enduring and unchanging Tao.
The name that can be named is not the enduring and unchanging name.
(Conceived of as) having no name, it is the Originator of heaven and earth;
(Conceived of as) having a name, it is the mother of all things.' And:
'I do not know its name, and I give it the designation of the Tao (The Way or Course).
Making an effort (further) to give it a name I call it The Great'.
Kia may also be related to the Qabalistic term Chia, Hebrew for 'life', and in the Qabalah,

the second highest essence of the human soul, corresponding to Chokhma (Wisdom).

14   Probably a reference to Crowley's *The Book of Lies* (1913), published in the same year as *The Book of Pleasure*, and which would have been in preparation at around the time Spare knew Crowley.

15   Spare seems to be describing what in N.L.P. would be called an 'unresourceful state': he advocates that we should be free to choose beliefs and make them our servants, rather than being enslaved to them.

16   Spare here attempts to syncretise Taoism with Qabalism. Several authors, including Crowley, have noted the many points of correspondence between the two systems.

In Crowley's words, 'The Yi King [a Taoist divinatory system] is mathematical and philo-sophical in form. Its structure is cognate with that of the Qabalah; the identity is so intimate that the existence of two such superficially different systems is transcendent testimony to the truth of both'.

Compare this passage in The *Book of Pleasure* to The *Tao-te Ching*:
'The Tao produced One; One produced Two; Two produced Three; Three produced All things'.

Tetragrammaton is a term borrowed from Qabalism, and represents the four-lettered name of God. It is composed of four Hebrew letters, Yod, He, Vav, He.

Each letter is assigned an element: Yod=Fire, He=Water, Vav=Air, second He=Earth.

Hence Spare has constructed a philosophical bridge between the Taoist account of the origin of all things, and the Four Elements from which, according to Western occultism, all things are made.

Spare has here set out an ontology (i.e. theory of the essence or origin of being) that is at odds with that of Aleister Crowley, who postulated in his *Berashith: An Essay in Ontology* (1902) that the dualities from which 'reality' is composed spring from absolute nothingness, an idea he later expressed in the equation $0=2$. Perhaps it is an awareness of this variance from the views of his erstwhile mentor that leads Spare to call his own theory 'unorthodox'. His insistence on the importance of 'Unity' is tantamount to Monism, the doctrine that the Universe is composed of one substance.

17   At the top of a letter to Kenneth and Steffi Grant of 16th October 1954, Spare lays out the 'Quadriga sexualis' (*Zos Speaks!* P105) as follows.

Five graphic sigils are laid out in a cross. The central one is unlabelled, but is a figure found frequently in Spare's work and symbolising 'I am I'.

From this figure and other information from *Zos Speaks!* the 'Quadriga sexualis' is as follows:

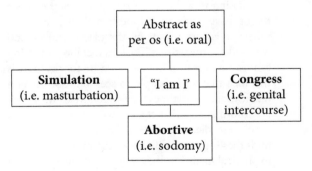

18   This passage seems to be alluding to the plotting
      of different aspects of existence onto the Qabalistic
      Tree of Life. The 'twelve-fold arrangement' does
      not make sense with respect to the conventional ten
      sephiroth, but Spare may be implying an additional
      two 'secret' sephiroth, one of which would be the
      'quasi-sephira' Da'ath. If he is, he would be neither
      the first nor last Qabalist to do so.

19   This symbol is evidently the 'first letter of the
      alphabet [of desire]' that appears a number of
      times in the artwork of The *Book of Pleasure*, thus:

20   From *The Tao-te Ching:*
      'The difficulty in governing the people arises
      from their having much knowledge. He who
      (tries to) govern a state by his wisdom is a
      scourge to it; while he who does not (try to) do
      so is a blessing'.

21   Again, 'New Thought'-style scepticism about
      science-based medicine: in other words, sick people
      go running to a doctor to 'save' them as they once
      might have gone to a priest: at least, much of
      medicine is very reliant on the placebo effect, and
      works like a superstition. The idea that life is suffering
      can lead to a fear of life and a desire for death. It is
      this idea that leads people to seek out doctors and
      medication, sometimes hypochondriacally. Frank
      Letchford relates that Spare was a great believer in
      home remedies and self-medication. If the reader
      finds these opinions difficult to accept with reference
      to physical medicine, they may find them easier with

respect to psychiatry: in his later *The Living Word of Zos,* Spare does indeed offer a critique of psychology and a theory of schizophrenia in terms that appear to anticipate R. D. Laing and the anti-psychiatry movement..

22   In other words, Death is not a finality, or a permanent state, but another illusion of consciousness, since the dead pass on to the astral plane and are not to be found among the living. If we believe in death as a final state, then we are practically dead now: and are blinded by our ignorance to the greater reality of Kia and Self-love.

23   Spare's argument here is related to Nietzsche's theory of Eternal Recurrence, but Spare adds the factor of 'decay' emphasising that everything repeats itself with slight variations: through the action of Kia, one version of the universe or idea of the self is realised, then destroyed, and another lightly different one is created. It is through these slight variations that consciousness arises. Spare speaks of the universe being destroyed daily, so perhaps he implies that the process is punctuated by sleep, dreams and death.

24   This passage is obviously inspired by the tale of Chuang-Tzu and the Butterfly:
'Long ago, a certain Chuang-Tzu dreamed he was a butterfly – a butterfly fluttering here and there on a whim, happy and carefree, knowing nothing of Chuang-Tzu. Then all of a sudden he woke to find that he was, beyond doubt, Chuang-Tzu. Who knows if it was Chuang Tzu dreaming a butterfly, or a butterfly dreaming Chuang-Tzu? Chuang-Tzu and butterfly: clearly there's a difference. This is called the transformation of things.'

From *Chuang Tzu: The Inner Chapters*, translated by David Hinton.

25   It is possible that this discourse about the Sun could have been inspired by Crowley's *Book Four* on Yoga. In it, Crowley writes, 'One of the simplest forms of Dhyana may be called "The Sun": the Sun is seen by itself, not by an observer, and although the physical eye cannot behold the Sun, one is compelled to make the statement that the "sun" is far more brilliant than the sun of nature. The whole thing takes place on a higher level' So in other words, the external form of the sun cannot be viewed directly, and in any case, is not as important as the internalization of its essential qualities.

26   Spare here seems to be introducing his concept of 'Atavistic Nostalgia' for the first time.

27   The original sentence contains a play on words: 'A thought for the sake of perspective – you are always what you most wish – the prospective'.

28   This passage seems to be a critique of 'The Law' of Thelema, expressed as, 'Do what thou wilt shall be the whole of The Law'.

    The title of The *Book of Pleasure* is probably intended as a riposte to Crowley's *Book of The Law*. To use an example from Crowley's *Diary of a Drug Fiend,* to say, 'It is my True Will to be an engineer and design a new type of helicopter' is an example put forward as 'True Will', but by believing in a True Will, we actually surrender any control we might have to it, and it becomes a separate entity (or 'sub-personality') dictating our every action. Thelema makes things unnecessarily complicated, and it does not take the whole outer order of the *Argentum Astrum*, a *Book of The Law*, or a *Religion of Thelema* to understand the Truth, which is simplicity itself.

29　The term 'Neither-Neither' seems to have been inspired by the Hindu yogic mantra, *neti neti*, meaning 'not this, not this', or 'neither this, nor that'.

It is held as the approach to understand the concept of *brahman* without using affirmative (and thereby inadequate) definitions or descriptions of *brahman*. Its purpose is to negate conscious rationalizations, and other distractions from the purpose of a meditation. Thus, the Divine is not real, nor is it unreal. It is neither living or dead, compassionate nor uncompassionate, and so on. We can never define God in words. Thus, it is making the same point as the *Tao-Te Ching* in saying that 'The name that can be named is not the true name' (see note 11). The 'Silent Watcher' becomes evident to anyone practicing meditation: one registers outside sense impressions, and realises 'I am not these sense impressions', one observes one's body, and realises 'I am not this body: it is my instrument and vehicle', one observes one's thoughts and emotions, and realises 'I am not these thoughts and emotions'. What one is left with is the Silent Watcher or Observer, a kind of blank recording mirror that registers things outside of itself, but which has no features of its own, and cannot look at itself. It can look both outside the body and inside the mind. In the Qabalah, this is the sephira *Tiphareth*, which is described thus by Will Parfitt: '*Tiphareth* is attributed to the centre of the whole person, the 'personal self', 'personal identity', 'ego', 'centre', or (sometimes) 'soul'. It is given many different names which are used by different people in different ways. For example, it is 'ego' in one sense of the word but not in another. For this reason, we prefer to attribute it to pure self-awareness, or quite simply the 'I'. Its planetary correspondence is the Sun.

30   Once again Spare is addressing an issue that will be familiar both to psychologists, and those practising meditation. Among the thoughts or 'ideas' that meditation allows 'The Silent Watcher' to observe with detachment, are false ideas about the 'self'. Someone who thinks of themselves as 'a calm person', can, under certain circumstances, become 'an angry person'. With practised detachment, the meditator can observe the belief that 'I am an angry person' as it comes into the mind, and decide whether to identify with it or not. If he does identify with it, it will acquire energy, and he will instantly become an angry person!

Alternatively, he may decide to ignore it, withhold energy from it, and allow it to pass and be replaced by calmer thoughts. The best way to deal with unwelcome thoughts is to accept them, not to take them seriously, and to neglect them. If we dwell upon them, we set up a conflict that keeps them supplied with energy, and thereby perpetuates them. The psychological concept of the 'sub-personality' is related.

31   Spare may be thinking of hermaphroditic creatures such as snails, and also certain fungi and protozoa in which there is conjugation between different 'strains' of an organism without externally apparent sexual differentiation. The theme of the androgyne was one that obsessed many late-nineteenth-century symbolist artists, and also Spare, whose

art contains numerous figures combining both male and female characteristics.

Spare's 'Neither-Neither' concept also seems to anticipate the post-modern philosophies of structuralism and deconstruction, as exemplified for example by Jacques Derrida. Briefly, deconstruction involves recognising binary opposites within a discourse (e.g. matter/mind, objective/subjective, object/representation, real/imaginary, external/internal, fact/fiction), then questioning the implied privilege, or status, given to one above the other. When these distinctions are reversed or blurred (as in much magical ritual) a liminal, or anti-structural condition is developed, in which the magician/trickster reigns. This seems to correspond to what Spare would later call the 'in-betweenness' concept. The magician/trickster has been personified in such mythical figures as Hermes, Thoth, and Loki: in short, this is the realm of both meaning and magic. See *The Trickster and The Paranormal*, by George P. Hansen (2001).

32   The method so far is a prescription for self-hypnosis leading to dissociation.

33   In a state of stillness and inner focus, it is indeed possible to discern 'an "X" in curious evolutions' amongst the phosphenes behind one's closed eyelids.

It forms the centre of the 'web' or 'tunnel' hallucination seen in drug and near-death experiences, and corresponds to the *Ajna* or Third Eye in Yoga.

34   It is unfortunate that Spare does not give more explicit instructions for the type of breathing he means: this passage is often interpreted as advocating overbreathing, but not only is this

potentially dangerous, but does not seem to be productive of useful effects. It is more likely to be holotropic, or 'connected' breathing, which is disinhibitory, and can produce a 'psychedelic' experience, utilized by 'rebirthing' practitioners.

35 Spare wrote more about the Death Posture in his late *The Zoetic Grimoire of Zos:* in the section *Sixth Formula: Metamorphoses by 'Death Posture' (by 'Zeno of Elea')* he writes: 'By means of the Death Posture, total transposition of consciousness into the sex-centre occurs. This brings about pure aesthesis and the creation of a new sexuality by autotelic concept: the subsequent ecstasy is sublimation. Because every other sense is brought to nullity by sex-intoxication, it is called the 'Death Posture'. Everything is *'a priori'* to the act. The *'a postiori'* illumination reveals the intersexual correspondences of all things, and great emotiveness becomes... My desires have made a sentient soul, an obsession, a vampire, an insatiable negress of pendulous breasts and fatted thighs riding me into the abysses of the quadriga sexualis...' In the later section, *Arbitrary Transference: illustration,* he writes: 'Indraw your breath until your body quivers and then give a mighty suspiration, releasing all your nervous energy into the focal point of your wish; and as your urgent desire merges into the ever-present procreative sea you will feel a tremendous insurge and self-transformation'. In a letter to Spare dated Sept. 10, 1954, Kenneth Grant asks 'Do you mean Sigh or is this word sigh just a parallelism (in your language) for Orgasm? This is, I take it, a variation of the Death Posture mentioned in

Bk. of Pleasure??' In his reply, Spare states, 'You are quite right in all your guesses. I deliberately used the word "suspiration"'as parallelism'.

36 In other words, at any moment, liberation is so close that the very act of asking the question is a procrastination that avoids an opportunity to jump out of time and experience it. Spare probably also has in mind the way institutionalised religion exerts its power over people by alienating them from religious experience and postponing it to an afterlife, accessible only on condition of compliance with church doctrine and priestly mediation. Mystics and Gnostics throughout the ages have always posed a potential challenge to this status quo, and have risked either persecution or reification by the church into   pedestallised 'holy' figures, whom ordinary people cannot hope to emulate (especially if they don't look too closely!) – see *Mysticism After Modernity* by Don Cupitt (1998); also *The Power of Now* by Eckhart Tolle (1999)).

37 "Emanation' may here be a euphemism for ejaculation.

38 Spare seems to be referring to the alchemical transmutation of sexual energy.

39 The 'Silent Watcher', or blank recording mirror, is common to everyone: see note (29) above.

40 In other words, we can add an edge of excitement, so we can feel like naughty little children again.

41 This passage could be construed as an anticipation of 'meme theory'.

42 In hermeticism (and church architecture) the element of Earth is represented by a bull. The elements are represented by the emblems of four beasts whose natures embody the underlying

essences of the elemental forces, namely, Lion (Fire), Eagle (Water), Angel (Air) Bull (Earth). (They are also associated with four Kerubic angels, Michael, Gabriel, Raphael and Uriel, as well as the four Evangelists, Mark, Matthew, Luke and John). The original illustrated *Book of Pleasure* contains four small vignettes of Spare's vulture-like Kia-bird, in different hybrid forms: a Lion/vulture, an Eagle/vulture, an Angel/vulture (which is also a Spare self-portrait/vulture!), and a Bull/vulture. It is also worth noting that in the word Kiā accompanying these vignettes, there is an accent on the 'A' confirming anecdotal information that Spare pronounced the word 'Ki-ah.' Also see note (15) above.

43   In other words, earthly life continues to evolve (thankfully) without the unhealthy meddling of human conscience.

44   Spare may have his own failed marriage in mind.

45   Also see note (36) above.

46   The 'six stupefiers': possibly adverse aspects of the six lower sephiroth.

From Will Parfitt's correspondence table:

Geburah:	Restriction
Tiphareth:	Pride
Netzach:	Lust
Hod:	Dishonesty
Yesod:	Idleness
Malkuth:	Inertia

47   Spare is referring to his own 'automatic' drawings. He is reported to have enjoyed spiritualist séances, yet seems to have remained a sceptic. Faked 'spirit photographs' depicting floating

double-exposed hands, heads and 'auras', and cheesecloth 'ectoplasm', were notorious at the time. Spare appears to have recognised them as fakery, yet used them as a point of departure for his symbolic art. Automatic drawing, directed by the unconscious, he recognised as a more genuine 'psychic' phenomenon.

48   The 'proto-zoa' depicted in the diagram 'Synopsis of Inferno' in Spare's *Earth Inferno* (1904) bear a certain resemblance to malarial parasites. Ronald Ross had described the transmission of malaria via mosquitoes in 1899, so the discovery would have been quite topical when Spare was compiling *Earth Inferno*, and he might have copied the figures from some scientific publication. Malaria (literally 'bad air') had in former times been attributed to malignant spirits.

49   A very prescient vision of twenty-first century humanity. At the turn of the year A.D. 2000, the Samaritans reported being inundated by callers distressed that they 'weren't enjoying the Millennium enough'.

50   In case you get bored and feel tempted to run away!

51   Monism again.

52   Compare the *Tao-te Ching*:
'The Uncarved Block, though seemingly of small account, is greater than anything that is under Heaven'.

53   *Tao-te Ching*:
'Banish human kindness, discard morality, and the people will be dutiful and compassionate'.

54   *Tao-te Ching*:
'Therefore the sage... learns to be without learning'.

In other words, instead of books and 'head-learning', we should learn to draw upon the vast resource of the unconscious mind that contains the memories of all our former existences, from which our instincts have developed. When a problem arises, we can be certain that we have encountered it before in another life, and the answer to it is held by our unconscious.

55 Again, compare the *Tao-te Ching*: 'Governing a large state is like cooking small fish'... in other words, the less they are poked about the better. If we try to proselytise to others, we are in danger of caring how they react, our well-being becomes contingent on their acceptance, and we 'lose our cool'. This attitude seems to prefigure Spare's later creed of 'Ecstoicism'.

56 See the first paragraph of 'Definitions'. Again, a possible reference to Spare's failed marriage.

57 See note (17).

58 Possibly another 'dig' at Crowley's *Book of The Law*: see note (28).

59 'Feast of the Supersensualists' is a phrase borrowed from Jacob Boehme. Spare adds his own footnote here, which reads, 'Chapter on self-attraction omitted'. This, like a number of other deleted chapters, seems never to have been written, but appears to have been intended for a second edition. A note at the end of Ernest H. R. Colling's introduction to the *Book of Pleasure* reads, frustratingly;

'NOTE In preparing this book for publication a few alterations have been found necessary at the last moment. In consequence, Daniel Phaer's introduction and portrait are omitted, together with the following chapters and corresponding illustrations, and the emblematic portraits of Ernest H.R.Collings: 'The Feast of the Supersensualists,' 'Modus Operandi at the Joy of the Round Feast,' 'Prophecy, Omens, etc.,' 'The Book of Revelation,' 'Definitions,' 'Dreams,' 'Mental States in Relation to Suggestion,' 'Description of Sensations and Emotions,' 'Controlling the Elements,' 'Black magic with Protection,' 'The Black Mass,' 'Vampirism,' 'Sorcery,' 'Oracles, etc.,' 'Superstitions,' 'Excitement to Love, etc.,' 'Use of Spells and Incantations on Men, Animals, etc,' 'Invoking Elementals, Nature Spirits for Glamour and Power, etc.' These may subsequently appear in a fuller edition.'

Several of the themes of these chapters, however, seem to have originated with Eliphas Levi.

60 'Organic' – i.e. genuinely and naturally felt: you really feel like it!

A misinterpretation of this passage may have led to the belief among 'chaos magicians' that a sigil needs to be 'charged' by gazing at it at the moment of sexual orgasm. Spare's original reads, 'Let him wait for a desire analogous in intensity… just a natural desire', and this seems to have been interpreted as a euphemism for the desire for sexual release. Although the desire spoken of may include sexual desire, it does not do so exclusively, and a close reading of Spare's text suggests that the process of submitting a sigil to the unconscious is an act of quiet meditation and sublimation of the 'free energy' of any disappointed desire of corresponding intensity and emotion. 'Charging' a sigil through sexual orgasm is unnecessary and is not without its disadvantages as a technique.

61 'Syllabub' – a dish made of cream or milk with wine etc. into soft curd… a sweet, delicious mixture!

62 The psychological ideas in this passage bear a strong resemblance to the Dissociation Theory of the pioneer psychologist and hypnotherapist, Pierre Janet (1859-1947). His ideas, together with those of Jean-Martin Charcot (1825-1893), aroused great interest among the early British psychical researchers of Spare's day, such as Frederic W. H. Myers (1843-1901), a founder member of the Society for Psychical Research. In his *Human Personality and Its Survival of Bodily Death* (1903), he became the first to introduce Janet's ideas to the English-speaking public, and treats of a number of themes that seem to be echoed in The *Book of Pleasure*, such as the nature of genius, hypnotism, automatism, and ecstasy.

63 Janet's Fixed Idea?

64 See note (5).

65 Stratified Fixed Ideas are another concept from Janet, being defined as resulting from traumata in the patient's life history that were sustained prior to the one which causes the full-blown hysterical or dissociative disorder.

66 Spare's term for unconscious belief is 'organic' belief.

67 Vacuity: when the conscious mind is quietened, and the unconscious is open to suggestion, eg in meditation or hypnosis.

68 Thus Sigil magic is seen by Spare as a way of deliberately exploiting Janet's mechanism of dissociation: the Sigil is made an 'Idee fixe' and is then made an unconscious, dissociated aspect of the personality by a process of deliberate repression, acquiring all the psychic power that that entails.

69   I have here kept to my policy of retaining the original sub-headings, but throughout the rest of the book I have changed 'sub-conscious' to 'unconscious'. Since Spare's day it has been realised that the term 'sub-conscious' has a pejorative ring to it that seems inappropriate in the light of the realisation of how great a thing the unconscious is in relation to the conscious mind: it is an amendment of which I am sure Spare himself would have heartily approved.

70   A characteristic of geniuses is that they often have some 'irrelevant' hobby to distract their conscious mind from the main task from time to time, so that their unconscious can work on it, and will later give them 'inspiration' at odd moments.

71   Compare with these passages in *Life and Matter: A Criticism of Professor Haeckel's Riddle of The Universe* by Sir Oliver Lodge (1905): ' "Parliament", or "the Army"... except as an idea in some sentient mind... could not be said to exist at all. The mere individuals composing it do not make it: without the idea they would only be a disorganised mob. Abstractions like the British Constitution, and other such things, can hardly be said to have any incarnate existence. These exist only as ideas.' (p.122)

'As to its technical continuity of existence and actual mode of reproduction, I suppose it would be merely fanciful to liken the 'Crown' to those germ-cells or nuclei, whose existence continues without break, which serve the purpose of collecting and composing the somatic cells in due season'. (p.123)

It is worthwhile taking a diversion here to consider the possibility of Ernst Haeckel (1834-

1919) having been at least an indirect influence on Spare.

Haeckel was a German biologist and evolutionary theorist, and in 1865 became professor of Zoology at the University of Jena. He was a passionate populist advocate of Darwin, and for this reason became known as 'The German Huxley'. He specialised in the study of marine invertebrates and protozoa, but his interests extended far beyond these. He is best known for his 'biogenetic law', which states that 'ontogeny recapitulates phylogeny', in other words, the development of the vertebrate (including the human) embryo reflects the evolutionary history of its species, so that, for example, at a certain stage of its development, a human foetus has a fish-like tail and gill-slits, and develops limb-buds in the same way as an amphibian. Haeckel held remarkably modern views on the continuity of life, the community between humans and other living creatures, and the 'essential unity of organic and inorganic nature'. He is credited with having coined the word 'ecology' (spelt 'oecology') in his book *The Riddle of The Universe* (published in English in 1900) Humans were not separate and different from the rest of nature. Everything in the cosmos, including all inorganic matter, and all life including humans, had material, energetic, and psychic aspects (the word 'psychic' was used interchangeably with 'psychological' at this time, and Haeckel states in *Riddle* that 'psychology is the study of the soul'). Even atoms had 'souls' of a kind – though by this, Haeckel only meant such principles as attraction, repulsion, crystallization, etc.

He states that, 'A long scale of psychic development ran unbroken from the lowest, unicellular forms of life up to the mammals, and to man at their head'. He proposed a future science of 'phylogenic psychology' tracing psychic functions from the 'crystal soul' or inorganic materials, through the primitive 'cell-soul' of the protista, up to the central consciousness of the higher vertebrates. (This would later provide a starting-point for Jung's theory of the collective unconscious).

Haeckel rejected the dualism which holds that matter and spirit are two separate substances, and developed his own philosophy of 'Monism'. He expounded what he called 'the Law of Substance', defined as 'the eternal persistence of matter and energy, their unvarying consistency throughout the entire universe'. He regarded matter and energy (within which he included the psyche) as 'two inseparable attributes of the one underlying substance', which took the place of God in his new religion. Haeckel's God was identical with the material universe, and human beings could relate to it through science (discovering its true nature) and through art (appreciating its beauty).

His other well-known book was *Kunstformen der Natur* or *Art-forms in Nature* (published in Germany 1904) which was a lavish picture-book of exquisite drawings of radiolaria, diatoms, sponges, jellyfish, and other creatures. In 1906 he launched the *Monistenbund*, or Monistic Alliance, to champion his new religion, and it gained a considerable following in Germany and Austria. However it later became associated with the eugenics and racial theorising that would come to underpin national-socialist ideology. It was this association, together with the scientific controversy surrounding his biogenetic law, that contributed to the subsequent decline in Haeckel's reputation, and the lapse into relative obscurity of this once-influential evolutionary theorist.

So what of Haeckel's influence on Spare? The *Riddle of the Universe* caused great excitement and consternation in Theosophical and Spiritualist circles on its English publication. Madame Helena Blavatsky attacked it, and Rudolf Steiner wrote a semi-sympathetic critique of it, based on lectures he had given in Austria (published in English as *Three Lectures on Haeckel and Karma*, in 1913, just too late to have influenced The *Book of Pleasure*, but Spare may have heard of the debate by reputation). There is no evidence that Spare read *Riddle of the Universe*, but he may well have read Sir Oliver Lodge's *Life and Matter: A Criticism of Professor Haeckel's Riddle of The Universe* (1905). It may just be coincidence that Haeckel uses the term 'self-love' in Riddle: 'The supreme mistake of Christian ethics, and one which runs directly counter to the Golden Rule, is its exaggeration of love of one's neighbour at the expense of self-love' (p.288, Thinker's library ed., 1929).

Haeckel's theories were not strictly Darwinian, but still influenced by the earlier evolutionary theorizing of Lamarck and Goethe.

Lamarck proposed the idea that creatures developed new limbs for new environments when they felt the need (and has, in recent years, received some unexpected vindication from modern studies of gene-switching). Goethe is known from other evidence to have been an influence on Spare. It is from this line of evolutionary theory that Spare may have obtained the formulation, 'the soul is the ancestral animals'.

In likening the floral motifs and precious stones of a crown to unicellular organisms, Spare might have had in mind some of the illustrations in *Kunstformen der Natur*, which although published in Germany, consisted mainly of pictures, and so was readily exportable: a copy may have made its way into Spare's hands, or he may have seen reproductions of the plates on display in the galleries of the London Natural History Museum, which Frank Letchford lists as one of the places Spare went to sketch. In any case, he certainly would have been able to see the Natural History Museum's collection of glass models of radiolaria, created by the German brothers Leopold and Rudolf Blatschka, based upon Haeckel's illustrations in *Die Radiolarien* (1862), and purchased by the Museum in 1876: they are mentioned in the Museum's *Gallery Guide* of 1907. (At time of writing, these extraordinarily exquisite and jewel-like models are the subject of a restoration project, with the promise of a large permanent display in the near future). His eye may have been especially drawn to these models, since the skeletons of some radiolaria display a geometry based on the five sacred Platonic Solids, and, as Kenneth Grant relates in *Images and Oracles*, whilst at school, Spare won a national gold medal for a 'treatise in Solid Geometry'.

(Some readers may be interested to know that Haeckel is also regarded as an influence on H. P. Lovecraft, who was known to have been an atheist and Monist: the evolutionary theories emerge occasionally in his stories, whilst the startling representations of marine life in *Kunstformen der Natur* appear to have provided some of the inspiration for his 'demons of the depths'. For those with eyes to see, one might speculate they could also represent a foretaste of Spare's 'primordial/new sexualities'!)

72 Again, there is no evidence that these 'missing chapters' were ever written.

However, there are some notes regarding dreams amongst Spare's later correspondence and manu-scripts published posthumously as *Zos Speaks!*

73 Original: 'righteousness'. From the context, it is clear that Spare intends 'right or wrong answers' in the academic, rather than the moral sense.

74 The mention of this incompletely-described 'true method' could be a fruitful area for occult speculation and experiment: it has hitherto received remarkably little attention from other commentators on Sigil magic.

75 Again, note the Janet-esque reference to a stratification of the unconscious.

In his excellent *The Artist's Books* (1995), Dr. William Wallace concludes from this passage,

'Sigils are all constructed in an identical manner and are formally similar. There must therefore be some other qualitative criterion for emphasis upon 'six methods of sigils'. The key appears to be within former allegories of *Earth: Inferno* and *A Book of Satyrs*, in which the role of the Microprosopus was highlighted. In its extended sense, the Microprosopus comprehends the six Sephiroth below Da'ath (excluding Malkuth) on the Tree of Life. Tiphareth is the hub of the singular ambit with action upon its satellite Sephiroth. Thus, the sigils are designed for the immediate purpose of referring a conscious desire to its appropriate Sephira.'

While there may be much in Wallace's theory of the six strata of the unconscious corresponding to the six sub-abyssic Sephiroth (say it six times quickly!), I submit that he misses the obvious point that there are clearly sigils constructed according to a number of different methods throughout the original illustrated *Book of Pleasure*, and one cannot conclude necessarily from Spare's vague language that 'sigils are all constructed in an identical manner and are formally similar'. The number of different types does indeed appear to be approximately six, and may be listed (tentatively) as follows:

- the Word Spell method (the one Spare has described here as an example);
- the Mantric Spell method (one that Wallace himself describes, though not recognising it as a type of sigil, *Op. Cit.* p.273);
- the Automatic Drawing method;
- the Chinese 'Cloud Drawing' method;
- the Pictorial/Symbolic method (described in the section headed 'Symbolism');
- the Geomantic method.

See *Practical Sigil Magick* by Frater U. D. (1990). I leave it to others to speculate over the correspondences these different methods may have with the six sub-abyssic Sephiroth.

76   The term 'Dwellers on the Threshold' originated in the novel *Zanoni* by Sir Edward Bulwer-Lytton, and was adopted by Theosophy. In occultism, the word 'Dweller' has a long history. H. P. Blavatsky used it specifically to mean 'certain maleficent astral Doubles of defunct persons'. However, it can have another meaning, referring to the imbodied

Karmic consequences or results of a person's past, haunting the thresholds which the initiate must pass before progressing to a higher degree of initiation. These dwellers can be defined as the imbodied quasi-human astral haunting parts of the psyche thrown off in past incarnations by the person who now has to face and overcome them.

'They are verily ghosts of the dead men that the present man formerly was, now arising to dog his footsteps, and hence are very truly called the karma-rupas of the man's past incarnations arising out of the records in the astral light left there by the "old" man who now is'. (From the *Collation of Theosophical Glossaries*.)

77 This 'thumbnail induction' is a classic technique of self-hypnosis: the 'moonbeam' need not be taken too literally: any subdued light will do. The thumb is stared at steadily whilst relaxing, until an opalescent 'aura' is seen around it – a symptom of hypnotic dissociation. It is the same process as attained by gazing into the pupils of one's eyes in a mirror as described for the 'Death Posture'.

78 But see *Two Tracts on Cartomancy* published by Fulgur Ltd., 1997.

79 Twenty-two is the number of paths on the Qabalistic Tree of Life. See Dr. Wallace for a detailed (if debated) study of Spare's Sacred Letters, which he sees as being at least partly based on Enochian.

80 Compare with *Earth Inferno*: 'I strayed with her into the path direct', referring to the 'Universal Woman', and according to Dr. Wallace, the central path of the Qabalistic Tree of Life.

81 Compare *Earth Inferno*: 'The convention of the age reaches its limit'.